L-Notes
By Brian Lennon

This book is dedicated to
GUIDANCE COUNSELLORS
who provide a very special service
to young people
and to their parents and teachers

Preface

Guidance counselling was my chosen career and continues to interest me in spite of retiring in 2009. After twenty-five years working as a guidance counsellor in St. Oliver's Community College, Drogheda, I then worked for five years as a psychologist with Co. Louth Vocational Education Committee.

During those last five years before retirement I noticed certain issues that arose in many of the ten education centres I visited weekly. One way of dealing with the more prominent of these matters was to prepare a short document about each and to email this to all the centres. I referred to these documents as "L-notes" ("L" for "learning") and they form the basis for this book. Also included are chapters about schemes we found useful in my own school experience. There is a certain amount of repetition in the hope of making each chapter reasonably independent.

In many cases these L-notes challenged traditional thinking about education and that is one of the aims of this book: to challenge, to find what is new and hopefully better, to grow. Growth always needs something new and the new can be challenging, sometimes uncomfortable. This challenge is not intended as a criticism of existing practices but simply as a way of exploring new and hopefully better ways to work. Another aim of these pages is to outline the practical details of some of the schemes we found beneficial to our students.

The experiences detailed in this book come from teaching in Ireland and our educational structures might not match those in other countries. For example, most young people both here in Ireland and in Britain progress from primary education to secondary education around the age of twelve. Such a transition has both advantages and disadvantages for the adolescents and meeting the needs of such a transition takes up several chapters in this book.

The ideas and practices described in these pages did not come from a single source and most were formed in the highly supportive and creative atmosphere of my school workplace, St. Oliver's Community College. I owe my fellow-teachers there a special thanks. They provided a student-centred environment where the true acid test of any new idea was how well it would help the students. The good people of historic Drogheda and its hinterland along the Boyne Valley formed the community I was privileged to serve.

Teachers and guidance counsellor colleagues working alongside me in St. Oliver's and in the other schools in Drogheda shared in many of the discussions that helped these ideas take shape. A special word of gratitude is owed to them. They are forever part of my family.

On a wider scale my colleagues in the Institute of Guidance Counsellors have always provided a wonderful forum for discussion, for learning and for support. In dedicating this book to guidance counsellors I naturally include this wonderful organisation.

Many thanks especially to friends and colleagues Arthur Dunne, Breeda Coyle, Jimmie Woods and Fred Tuite who made valuable comments about the draft manuscript. Thanks also to Tom Farrell for his great support.

One particular guidance counsellor played a special role in the development of these ideas. He was the outgoing holder of the post I filled in 1974 and later became my principal, my CEO and always my friend, Eamon Cooney. Without his vision, initiative and support many of these ideas would never have seen the light of day.

For the past thirty years sailing friend Frankie Browne has asked me, "When are you writing another book?" Here you are Frankie … and thanks for the encouragement!

In 1985 I first learned about Dr. William Glasser's Reality Therapy. His ideas on counselling greatly enriched my own approach to helping young people and his explanation of Choice Theory psychology opened up many new understandings of how education might work. The reader will find many of his influences throughout these pages.

Finally, as always I owe so much to my wife Laura. She backed me up through my studies until I got my first guidance counselling job and she has been so supportive of all my informal studies since then. She is the love and light of my life.

Brian Lennon
Guidance Counsellor

Prologue

This is a book that can be dipped into at any point, the only real connection between the chapters being their common theme of education and development of young people. Some chapters address counsellors and teachers directly, others are intended for student use in the form of handouts or advice from teachers. The patchwork quilt distribution of chapters is a reflection of the origins of these ideas in separate articles.

In the text I use "he", "she" and even "he or she" but at all times what I write applies to all sexes and genders. Similarly, when I refer to parents I include step-parents, foster parents and guardians.

Hopefully these pages will provide you with new angles on old ideas and new ideas on old angles. I would be quite surprised if you agreed with everything in the book but hopefully it will inspire you to explore new directions.

Although the chapters focus a lot on the role of the guidance counsellor, I would hope that the contents are of interest to all educators and especially to those who provide a school-wide support service such as home school community liaison personnel, school completion people, principals and deputy principals.

It is over thirty years since I published my first book ("The Career Handbook") and I would hope that this volume conveys some of the experience of the intervening years. However, it would be a mistake to assume that the future will be a replica of the past. The speed of technological and social change is breathtaking and the world we are preparing young people for is one that none of us over the age of twenty-five knows very well. Hopefully, as you read through these pages you will think of new ways to advance the service we as educators provide to those young people.

The book does not attempt to cover every possible area. For example, in my own school we developed approaches to Pastoral Care, Sex and Relationship Education, Personal Wellbeing, Bullying and Anger Management as well as Career Guidance programmes. These topics have not been included here. Important parts of the guidance counsellor's role are counselling and career guidance but these are barely mentioned here as I have contributed to these area elsewhere in my career textbooks and software or in books currently in preparation.

An important emphasis is that on whole-school guidance and the topics include here reflect the goal of reaching all students and not simply school-leavers. Extra space is given to the early years since a firm foundation is essential in any project and education is no exception.

Where some typical student stories and problems are presented throughout the book, names and other details do not represent specific real persons. Where authors are mentioned a reference to at least one of their works is included at the end.

The self-contained nature of most of the chapters in this book make it suitable as background material for discussion groups or supervision groups. Each member of the group could read the chapter in advance of the meeting and then there is a general discussion at the meeting. Alternatively, one member reads the chapter, summarises it to the group and then have the discussion.

If I could choose how you read this book I would recommend your taking one chapter at a time. Read and re-read it, tease out the ideas, challenge them, create your own views about the topic.

However you use the book I do hope it will inspire new ideas and directions in the exciting and ever-changing world of education.

Table of Contents

Welcoming New Students

Unlike most other jobs, those in education face a large influx of new "clients" every year. There is an inevitable degree of confusion for everyone until the dust settles and both sides get to know each other a little better.

In the staff-room, teachers compare notes about their new class groups and the new faces they see there. There are children who are wonderful, highly motivated, hard workers, models of good behaviour ... and then there are the others!

They "don't like criticism"; they "don't take correction easily". They have poor concentration, get restless. Some are often absent or late (meaning they would rather be somewhere else). Others can be lazy (meaning they prefer an easier way of doing things). A lot seem to lack motivation (meaning they are motivated but not to do what we want them to do)!

Then there are children from homes that are topsy-turvy for one reason or another. It could be due to a serious illness, a bereavement, a recent separation, someone in prison, poverty, a total lack of interest or just very poor parenting skills or, indeed, a host of other factors. They come to school often unwillingly and in different states of readiness (physical, psychological and academic).

But isn't our job only to teach them subjects? Aren't there specialist staff members in schools to deal with the student's overall development? Don't we need to ensure that those kids who are really interested get a decent education?

The problem is that work with young people is not so easily compartmentalised! Nobody who works with kids "only" teaches their school subject. Like it or not and for better or worse we form part of their holistic education as human beings. Even if we do not want to influence them they are still learning general life-skills from us. There is no escaping that and so we need to be clear about just how we influence our students at a personal level.

This applies especially to those young people who can make life difficult in the classroom. A principal I hold in high regard once said to me, "when I feel most like throwing them out I know that's when they need us the most". The fact is that those who do not fit into our educational system so well are those who are in most need of it. If we as their educators do not make an effort to help them develop it is likely that society will pay the price later on. It is equally likely that these young people will have unhappy lives and, sadly, have offspring who will continue this process of marginalisation.

So many of these young people can so easily and so quickly get on the "wrong side" of teachers, especially those kids who have never been anywhere else in the past. We as teachers have a golden opportunity to make a difference. Our Irish educational system sees fit to have most twelve-year olds get a fresh start in a completely different school system.

Such a transition has its drawbacks but one major advantage is that the student can have a fresh start. But, be warned, fresh starts don't happen automatically. In fact we need to become experts in fresh starts, knowing how to give the "worst" students a break they never expected. A warm personal welcome to all your new students is a good beginning and a great rule of thumb, a welcome that is offered before any trouble can brew … or be brewed!

This works both ways: it is good for the student and it is good for the teacher. Establishing a sound relationship from the very first minutes makes it much easier to relate to that student in later weeks and months. It even becomes easier to help the student integrate better into the school.

Another important thing we can do is to make our subjects interesting to students. I have great respect for what I call the "BBC approach" to education. The British Broadcasting Corporation seems to have developed the knack of presenting a programme about anything, even the scavenging habits of sewer rats, and make it compulsive viewing! If our way of presenting the syllabus is attractive to our students, they will want to learn and children who are engrossed in learning tend to have neither the time nor the inclination to be disruptive.

A great book full of ideas in this regard is "The Teacher's Toolkit" by Paul Ginnis. Another book every teacher should have and read is "How to Talk so Kids can Learn at Home and School" by Adele Faber and Elaine Mazlish. For example, it has a section about "praise that doesn't demean and criticism that doesn't wound".

At the heart of the above approaches is the Choice Theory psychology idea that we simply cannot control another human being! This applies to partners, parents, children, colleagues ... and students! We can influence them if we get the relationship right. Staying calm and knowing what to do is a big part of that.

Above all our students need to know (and not simply be told) that we are on their side. Getting the qualification to teach was the easy bit; the constantly changing human interaction is the real challenge of education!

This chapter is highlighting the general approach that is needed. The specific details are listed in following chapters. Some teachers are wary of attempting a positive relationship with students as they do not know how to be firm and fair at the same time. All three components (friendliness, firmness and fairness) are vital to the teaching relationship but the "how" of such a connection needs to be explored.

Transition to Secondary School

It is a characteristic of the education system throughout Ireland and some other countries that many children move from primary schools to secondary schools around the ages of 11 or 12. Any such transition from one school to another can be quite traumatic for many children as it can bring many changes:

- A farewell to the familiar world of primary school
- Less contact with original school pals
- Going from the top of one ladder to the bottom of another
- New friendships
- New school start and finish times
- Longer school day
- Changed meal times
- Different transport to school
- Greater number of students and staff
- Responsibility for a locker, keys and passes
- Initiation into the teen subculture
- Changes in dress code in and out of school
- New rules and regulations
- For some a boarding school experience
- New gender balance in classmates
- New strengths and weaknesses to discover
- Increase in number of subjects
- Increase in the number of text-books used (and size of school-bag)
- More examinations
- Possible change in class placement ranking
- Multiplicity of teachers and teaching styles
- Regular room changes and a timetable to follow
- Addition of specialist members of staff
- Probably a bigger selection of sports and clubs
- Often a greater number of ethnic groups
- Possible changes in religious or secular ethos of the school

- In some cases a new language of daily communication

Not only is the educational environment changing but the child's own personal world is facing into puberty with all the hormonal and mood swings that accompany it. New social awareness and relationships appear and all of this is later complicated even further by sexual attraction, self-concept and gender identity issues. Parents and guardians can be caught off-guard by all these changes where their little swan seems to be re-emerging as an ugly duckling instead of the other way around.

To leave such children to their own devices would be bordering on neglect. It is here that the specialist services of guidance counselling, home school community liaison and school completion are particularly important. It is also vital that all staff offer a positive and welcoming environment to the young people in their care.

There are essentially four types of student as far as transitions are concerned. (1) There is the main body of students who move from one environment to the other with no major problems. (2) There are those who were flourishing in the primary school and unexpectedly find themselves in deep water in the secondary system. (3) There are students who stumbled through primary and, somehow or other, find themselves thriving in the secondary environment. (4) There are those who were finding things difficult in primary and the difficulty seems to follow them into secondary.

Some advance knowledge about these new arrivals would be a boon. However, primary school teachers are often justifiably reluctant to provide secondary schools with information about their outgoing pupils. They prefer to see their students move forward with a "clean slate", ready to start afresh. The problem with this admirable thought is that children with existing behavioural problems are likely to display these in their first hours in the new school and get off to a bad start with their new teachers. The clean slate can be very lucky to survive the first morning. Withdrawn children can be overwhelmed completely in the first hours and their distress can go totally unnoticed for a long time.

Behavioural problems can range from highly visible hyperactivity and disruption to the more invisible personal problems such as shyness and inner turmoil. These are all conditions that can benefit from some external support during the first days at the new school but for this help to be fully effective it is necessary that the support services have advance information about the problems. This is not always easy to obtain.

Advance contact with the feeder schools is the first step and it is important that those who engage in this contact establish a high level of trust with the primary school staff. If you are making this contact it is important to inform the primary teachers of the level of confidentiality you will afford to any information received and to tell them exactly what you will do with that information.

In my own experience we did not pass on specific details about a student's problems to other staff. Instead we would identify children that might have difficulties and then recommend tutors and year heads to give them a special welcome without going into details of the child's issues. In some cases we would create special new school experiences for the incoming students. It is important for the primary teachers to know about such an approach and learn to trust it.

Another facet of incoming students that proved important was to know about their strengths. A child who had built up a reputation in primary school for great ability on the sports field or in the art room would benefit from speedy recognition of these talents in the new school. We established a general approach to dealing with specific groups of incoming pupils.

Disruptive behaviour: Our aim was to create positive experiences of the new school as soon as possible. Their tutors and teachers would be recommended to provide a warm welcome to these individuals and to relate to them as early as possible.

Withdrawn children: Here we would make sure to establish brief contact on the first day and to follow this up by gradually increasing interactions. Any special talents would be used to help link the child to like-minded students in the new school as soon as possible. The child's new teachers would be alerted to the need to avoid spotlighting the child and to include them in classroom activities very gradually.

Talented kids: Relevant staff would be told about these talents and recommended to mention these to the child as soon as possible.

Unique talents or interests: After establishing contact with the child, the guidance counsellor would create a new club or one-shot club (detailed in another chapter) so that this young person would integrate fully with the secondary school.

High achievers: This group could have special challenges in the new school. A pupil who was accustomed to coming top of the class in primary where there were around 25 children per class could now find that his or her new class ranking was seriously reduced in a school of over 200 new students. This could result in a serious blow to the student's self-esteem. Shortly after the first week a brief chat with the student and open discussion about rankings could help the child assimilate the new environment.

Health issues: information about specific health problems or allergies would be circulated discreetly to all staff dealing with these children. Where necessary an information sheet about how to deal with specific health issues would be circulated.

Most of the above information could be obtained in carefully managed meetings with primary school staff in the term before the new school year begins. Such data collection can be carried out by the guidance counsellor, the home-school community liaison person, the school completion person or a combination of these. What is important is that all such information is collated and leads to specific plans of action.

Enrolment Tests

Other helpful information about new students can be gained from well-chosen enrolment tests or similar information provided by the primary school. The child's current level of achievement in literacy and numeracy is very important as such information allows the secondary school to plan any remedial interventions that may be needed.

A measure of general knowledge helps reveal how well the child tunes into the world around.

Measures of the child's intelligence in verbal reasoning, numeric reasoning and perceptual reasoning can be useful in highlighting discrepancies between ability and achievement. Such discrepancies warrant further investigation to identify and deal with the underlying causes. The tests chosen for this purpose must be reliable and valid as measures of ability. (Note that strong verbal reasoning is not an indication of aptitude for foreign language learning.)

It is vital that such tests have adequate floor and ceiling for the population they are used to assess. If the resulting curve of scores is heavily skewed towards low or high scores, the measuring instrument is suspect. Not only are such tests of dubious value but there is a strong likelihood that they either frustrate or bore the students who take them.

The use of and, equally important, an informed understanding of the nature of standard scores is needed. The data used for standardisation must come from a relevant sample population and the samples used must be large enough to create valid standardisation formulae. If comparisons of an individual's scores on different tests are to be made (e.g., intelligence with reading ability), then the standardisations need to be similar.

To say that a particular student has an IQ score of 115, and a reading score of 22 is meaningless, useless and potentially misleading unless we know more about the nature of these scores. If 115 represents one standard deviation above the mean for the IQ test (a "z" score of +1) and the reading score is also one standard deviation above the mean, then we can be reasonably confident that this child's reading is on a par with ability.

Where there is a discrepancy between the scores, this could be due to the accuracy of the tests used ("standard error of measurement") but it is safe to say that any difference of one standard deviation or more is worth exploring further. From the above it should be clear that it is worthwhile expressing all the tests scores in one common standardised form such as "z-scores" or "t-scores". Otherwise comparison is not easy.

In a given class grouping two students might have the same IQ, say, 110. Standardised scores like these can give rise to misunderstandings about ability. Mary is

11.9 years of age and her raw score of 27 converted into a standard score of 110. Peter, on the other hand, is 12.5 years of age and his raw score of 35 converted into a standard score of 110. Both students have the same IQ score. However, the reality of the situation is that these two students who now sit together in the same class had quite different raw scores in the same test. This raw score rating is much closer to the reality that Mary and Peter's teachers will be observing rather than the standardised scores derived from them. On the other hand, Mary's lower raw score could lead to an inaccurate underestimation of her ability. An understanding of the strengths and weaknesses of both raw and standardised scores is essential.

In short, a study of both raw and standard scores is needed for any test data interpretation that is to be useful to a school (rather than to educational administration where the agenda can be quite different). Within a school the guidance counsellor is in the best position to scan the data of incoming students and to interpret the test profiles of each student. The guidance counsellor can be helped greatly in this task by the local educational psychologist.

Given that different schools will use a wide variety of tests, it is impossible to give precise pointers as to their use and interpretation. However, here are some general guidelines to interpreting the student profiles. In all cases it is assumed that standardised scores from the same background population are being used.

- Do any of the test scores in an individual profile show a discrepancy with the rest (e.g., one standard deviation or more) and, if so, what is the likely cause and remedy?
- Does a discrepancy between verbal and non-verbal tests point to difficulties in verbal reasoning rather than in overall ability?

- Does a low verbal reasoning score combined with high scores in other scales suggest a poorly developed linguistic code and/or reading skills?
- Do raw-score differences with classmates suggest any areas of difficulty for the student?
- Do the child's primary teachers agree with the results of the enrolment test and, if not, can they shed light on the differences?

Of course, transition to a new school is not simply about behavioural and academic reports. Some type of organised induction to the new environment is virtually a necessity. This can take the form of sessions during the holidays before the term begins or special meetings on the first days of term or even a combination of both. An approach to induction will be the subject of a later chapter.

A Clean Slate or a New Leaf

Wayne and Natasha have three things in common: one, both hated their primary school experience; two, in both cases their primary schools are relieved to be rid of them and three, both are now sitting in your class in their first day at second level!

With Wayne it all started early on. Even at age five Wayne would sometimes steal other students' lunch treats or even their lunch money. When his parents were notified they either did not respond at all or came to the school in a defiant mood. They would say that "other children did the same as Wayne but weren't picked on" and "it was all because the teacher didn't like Wayne." Of course it did in fact become increasingly difficult for the teachers to like Wayne. This pupil spelt trouble at every possible level. His teacher watched him constantly because she needed to.

Natasha's story was different. Until the age of eight she was a regular pupil, neither a star nor an imp, just coasting along in the middle of the class group. She always did her work and was careful about her appearance. Then there was a dramatic change. She started getting into constant fights with other students. This led to punishment from her teacher and in a short space of time Natasha had been identified as a very difficult pupil. As she got into her final years at primary she started smoking, began hanging around with older girls and then older boys. More than once in her final year the teacher had to remind Natasha not to be speaking about her evening escapades in school.

Wayne had grown up in a home with eight siblings. His parents knew little about how to bring up kids although they did care for them and prided themselves on standing by them. Both food and money were in short supply and tempers tended to be short also. The only way Wayne knew how to get by was to fight his corner.

The more he fought, the more he needed to fight ... and the more corners he found in his life. As the adult world appeared more and more threatening he found safety and comfort in the company of like-minded kids, kids who lived on the fringes of society.

Natasha had only one little brother and her parents were very loving towards the children. However in the new school year that coincided with Natasha's ninth birthday it was a more sullen child that dragged her heels to school for the first day of term. Just a month previously a younger cousin of her Dad's had come home from abroad and stayed with them for two weeks. He was twenty. Natasha reached her birthday that year with a dark secret she was not supposed to tell. Without adult help a child of eight knows little about dealing with such things and the resulting pain and confusion overflowed into her behaviour. Her increasingly wild friends helped her forget the suffering.

Now Wayne and Natasha are in your class. So too are Rita, Grainne, Tom and Fran but their stories would take too long. So what can you do? Many teachers believe in giving their new students a totally clean slate. It must be said that this is incredibly effective ... for at least thirty minutes! The problem with the clean slate is that there's nothing on it!

By the time these young people have finished a brief stock-taking exercise of you they revert to what they are familiar with and use their established ways for dealing with a school environment! On the other hand, if we as teachers have a plan, things have a good chance of working out differently. These kids need a new leaf, a new beginning! That means something has to be different - and you can make it so.

First Day at the New School

The very first moments of contact with new students are incredibly important and need to be planned very carefully. I cannot emphasise enough that "first moments" really does mean first moments, measured in minutes rather than in hours. As a guidance counsellor I believed in monitoring very closely the first hour of the new students' time in the school and providing special support to the teachers of that hour.

In the first day's first moments ….

- Give priority to identifying the new students by name.
- Have short lists of the priority cases.
- As the students are called out into their class groups match names and faces as soon as possible.
- When the class group assembles for the first time to be brought off to their first classroom session, chat informally with them and give a little extra attention to the priority students.
- With students who have been reported to you as extremely withdrawn keep your initial contact to a minimum. (e.g., "What is your name?" "Good to meet you!")
- With students who have been reported for behavioural problems give them a special warm friendly welcome, wishing them a successful time in their new school. Chat about any interests you think they might have or ask them about their interests. Let them see a smiling face! They are not used to such!

Now for some examples! These are based on real cases but, as with all the examples in this book, the details have been changed completely to protect their identities. These sample stories point to the importance of intervening as early as possible in the new student's first hours in the school.

Louise had been described as extremely withdrawn, as a child who put up barriers to all communication. My first encounter with her was just after hearing her name and class group called out. As I moved along the line of waiting students I greeted her simply by asking her name and saying, "Welcome to the school". She nodded a little but kept her eyes firmly fixed on the floor. I moved quickly to the next student.

In subsequent days I would greet her with a smile in the corridors but deliberately did not stop to talk. After a few weeks I risked a conversation by asking her what she was interested in. She muttered something about midi files, her face and eyes still directed at the floor throughout the brief conversation.

A few days later I met Louise on the corridors and I spoke to her about another student in her year group who was also interested in midi files and who knew how to find lots of them on the Internet. Her head raised with open eyes. Interest! Would she like this chap to show her how to find the files? She nodded in a way that showed she did not have much practice at nodding!

The boy was one I had chosen carefully as an equally quiet child but quite skilled with computers. (This was in the days when computers were still quite a novelty.) A number of shared sessions sitting at one of the school computers resulted. From this point on Louise made good progress and this was enhanced by a small music club that was specially created to nurture her interest. Before she left the school she had won a competition with one of her midi files. She now works as a specialist with a computer company.

Johnny Cantwell's case was quite different! It was clear from the primary teacher's description of Johnny that trouble was on the horizon. He had been disruptive, argumentative and very challenging in his primary school. In fact I had not recalled hearing a more negative report about any new student. His surname caught my attention as we had one teacher with that name in the school and that gave me the idea for a plan. I shared my scheme with the teacher in advance and he agreed to it as I thought he might.

When greeting the class group I arrived at Johnny's position. "Hello, what's your name?" "Johnny, sir!" "And your second name?" "Cantwell, sir!" "OK, follow me!" A surprised and increasingly worried Johnny followed a very non-chatty me along the school corridors until I reached Mr Cantwell's office. Johnny, well used to being in trouble, showed all the signs of a dead man walking. We knocked on Mr. Cantwell's door and entered.

The teacher asked what the problem was and I replied, "You are a Cantwell and this chap is a Cantwell too. We have too many Cantwells here!" The teacher stretched out his hand to Johnny saying, "Don't you worry! We Cantwells have to stick together!" To the amazement of his primary teachers, Johnny never gave us the slightest bit of trouble in the school and none of the new school teachers, with the exception of Mr. Cantwell, ever learned what challenges they had missed! In seconds we had been able to dispel Johnny's view of school as a hostile place and open up the possibility of his starting afresh.

Then there was Mike. According to his primary teacher Mike was always getting into fights. He was big for his age and pushed his weight around a lot getting into many scraps. But Mike had a secret side. His family situation was complex and he often had to look after his ailing father, something he did with admirable care. Just after hearing his story from the primary principal I asked if I might "borrow" Mike. The principal called him to the office and asked Mike if he would help carry some equipment up to his future school. Mike agreed, probably glad of an opportunity to get out of class.

When we arrived at the other school I thanked him and then asked him if he had seen around the place. He had not. Would he like a quick tour? He would! That was all there was. In September Mike was coming to a school he knew better than his peers and he had already met some of the staff on very friendly terms. Mike had an uneventful passage through his secondary education.

It is cases such as these that help build the relationship with the feeder schools. They gradually realise that the transition from one school to another is indeed a chance to start with a clean slate but this chance needs the support of teachers from both schools. A clean slate is possible if it is well planned.

There is one little drawback to this approach. Your fellow teachers will never really get to appreciate the effectiveness of this approach as they will know nothing of the child's previous track record. The new leaf can become a very clean slate.

The Induction Programme

For a number of years St. Oliver's had brought in the new first year students on their own so that the building would be less crowded and school-life less complex on their first day at their new school. Initially they had a first session in the morning with their class tutor and then the rest of the day was according to the timetable. At some point in the nineties we realised that it would be worthwhile to spend the whole day with a specially prepared induction programme.

The primary aim of this approach was to help the students get to know their new surroundings in such a positive way that they would actually want to come back on the second day. If this sounds like a simple objective just imagine the impact on a student's life where he or she does not want to come back.

In advance of the first meeting, the guidance counsellor fed information to the class tutors about students who might need special attention (averaging one to three per class) and the aim was to help those students feel especially welcome. No specific details about a student's personal problems were released. The year head and tutors involved in the running of the induction day were given special training in advance and a set of notes to guide them through the first day. Peer counsellors were also employed in this programme and they too received special training.

General guidelines at the beginning of the Induction Day notes

- First impressions are very important.
- You might be someone's first impression of us.
- A friendly environment will bring out the best in everyone.
- Offer greetings, smiles and respect.

- Volunteer contact with new students, don't wait for them to approach you.
- Watch out for those who are on their own or who look a little confused. Chat with them and if possible link them to other students.
- Ask new students about their names, where they come from, how they feel about the new school, what they are looking forward to the most.
- Where there are minor behavioural problems offer an alternative in a friendly and cooperative spirit.
- Report extreme behaviour to the Year Head promptly.

General Assembly

All new students are gathered in the Assembly Area and are formally welcomed to the school by Principal and Deputy Principals.

The list of names of each class grouping is called out and the group then goes off with their Tutor to have their first class together.

Each first year class group stays in the same room for most of the day. This reduces the confusion of having many new students trying to find their way around a new building at the same time.

The first session is led by the class tutor and the following advice is provided about dealing with the special students:

Your attention may be drawn to certain new students who could have some special difficulty settling into the school. Problems may arise due to personality, behaviour or academic standards. ALL students will benefit enormously from a positive introduction to the school but some students need to get this message loud and clear in their first hours here. If you are notified about special students, please give them extra time and attention.

Here are some ideas on how to do this:

- Establish positive contact with each of these students. (See ideas on this page and the following one on the first session.)
- Do this as early as possible on the first day.
- Be unobtrusive.
- Give positive affirmation for anything you can. ("You look very well in the uniform." "Your handwriting is very clear." "You look like you could be a good boxer." "Where did you get such a good school-bag?") This can be done very effectively whilst the class is working on something and you comment quietly to a specific student.
- Chat with the student about where they are from, what sports or hobbies they like, etc. This may be done inside or outside the classroom. If you find out any special strengths or interests note these down and share them at the tutor meeting.
- Give the student some small responsibility - clean the board, do a message, etc. (Tone this down in the case of very reserved students.)
- Create situations where they can be successful easily and receive genuine praise. That is, set the student up for success.

If you wish to discuss any of the points raised here, please contact the guidance counsellor. If you notice other students in your class who may have special difficulties (health, personality, behaviour, etc.), please jot down their names and pass them to the guidance counsellor later on.

Notes for the first session by the Tutor

Your very first session with your tutorial group should aim at establishing one thing and one thing only: "INVOLVEMENT". This means establishing a good relationship, one that can be described as "professional friendship". Here are some ideas which may be helpful:

Issue all new students with their school journal emphasising in a positive way that they are now officially students of this school.

1. Give your own name ... ask the students to write it down in their Journal. (You may wish to personalise this more by giving more details about yourself, maybe memories of your own first day at secondary school.)

2. Briefly explain your role as Tutor.

- you are a special teacher assigned to this class
- you will meet the class once a week
- you will deal with some topics to do with their life in general
- you want to hear their ideas, their opinions
- if they have special problems they can discuss these with you

3. Explain any basic ground rules you wish to use in the class.

4. Chat with the class:

- Where are you from?
- How many have brothers or sisters here already?
- What was hardest for you this morning so far?
- Did anything funny happen to anyone here today?
- What do you hope will be different about this school?
- Who does not know anyone else in this classroom?

5. Explain that they will stay in the same room for most of the day and that different teachers will give them information about the school.

Your first session with the class should finish just before the morning break and, just before you go, explain how long the break is and tell them where the nearest toilets are, usually a priority in a new environment!

During the morning break the specially trained peer counsellors would be available to help the new students find their way around, locating the toilets and seating areas and ensuring that they could find their way back to the Induction Day classroom.

Other Induction Day Topics

Subjects: brief descriptions of the subjects available, the compulsory subjects, the elective subjects. There could be some discussion to offset gender bias in subject selection. A brief outline of the State examination system would be given.

School Layout: Every student is given a map of the school and some explanation of its layout. They are told about emergency exits, about where their buses arrive and depart, where they can park bicycles, what areas are available for breaks and having lunch, where the toilets are, special details for students with specific disabilities. Even in advance of the first fire drill it is vital to tell the new students that if they hear the fire alarm they should move quietly to the nearest exit and move at least 50 metres from the school building. The explanation is followed by a brief guided tour of the school where all the main features are pointed out. Later in the day we often had a school "treasure hunt" with items such as "What colour is the principal's door?", "What office is right beside the guidance counsellor's office?", "How many tennis courts are beside the car-park?" The aim was to help the students become familiar with key locations on the campus. The peer counsellors would help in these walking activities.

Practical Matters: This session deals with topics such as the timetable, protecting personal property, storage lockers, who to approach about specific problems (permission to leave the building, reporting back after absence, being sick, missing the bus, lost and found, being bullied, general worries, interest in joining or starting a club).

School Rules: Essentially in St. Oliver's there was only one rule, "RESPECT", and the details of this were teased out with the group. Students were encouraged to explore the whole idea of rules, what school or society would be like without them. The new students were told how the school staff would deal with breakdowns in rules. They were also told that specific subjects (e.g., Physical Education) would have their own rules.

Preparation for the Next Day: The last session in Induction Day was devoted to a detailed preparation for the next day - What to wear and what to bring to school, where the first class would take place. At the end of this last session, the teacher would bring the group to their exit and departure point in the school so that they would know the route for the next day.

A lot of information is supplied to new students during the induction programme. It is vital that this is shared in a friendly way otherwise it can be perceived as overwhelming and even threatening. By the end of the first day each new student should feel more confident about the new surroundings and should be looking forward to the next day. Their secondary education has been well and truly launched!

Peer Counsellors

Some schools operate a fully fledged peer counsellor scheme where senior students are available all the year round as supports to other students. We developed a simpler model of this aimed mainly at the integration of first year students into the school.

The role definition of these peer counsellors is:

- To be available throughout the new students' first day in the school.
- To assist in some of the classroom exercises run by teachers on the first day.
- To be available at break-times during the first week of term.
- To be clearly identified to new students as people they could approach for help.
- To be on the outlook for students who had problems of any sort.
- To help direct students around the building.
- To deal with basic questions about the school.
- To know when to refer issues to school staff.

This service is in no way a substitute for staff supervision but the scheme provides a new layer of support between staff and junior students. Apart from its specific benefits to new students this service had several other advantages:

- It offers those who volunteered for the scheme an opportunity to help others.
- It helps them learn some elementary counselling skills.
- It provides experience of collaboration between staff and students.
- It strengthens general bonds between students and staff.

- The peer counsellors gain first-hand evidence of the school's caring dimension by participating in it.
- The role provides useful experience to those considering careers in any support service.
- It is a valuable addition to the young person's CV.

Preparation begins the previous school year in the spring term by inviting volunteers to a meeting. The volunteers are sought from the ranks of transition year students since they have two consecutive years without state examinations. The role is described in detail at the meeting so that the students are fully aware of what they are volunteering for. This initial meeting is followed up by a training day which sometimes takes place at a venue outside the school.

Here is a sample of the topics covered in the training day:

- Role description of a peer counsellor.
- Basic listening skills.
- How to facilitate bonding exercises to help the students develop team spirit.
- Knowing the answers to standard questions from new first years.
- Training in the exercises they will participate in with the new students.
- Learning about what situations are to be referred to staff.
- Outline of the events of the first day and week of the coming term.

This training is carried out by the guidance counsellors and class tutors of the incoming first-years.

On the first day of the new school year these peer counsellors have a special briefing session about 30 minutes before the first event gets underway.

Developing Interests

Many young people seem to develop their interests from early childhood experiences. Their parents and teachers encourage them to participate. Very often a new experience begins with an awkward phase and it is only with support and encouragement from parents or teachers that the young person perseveres. They then establish the beachhead where the activity's own inherent satisfaction reaches them.

From that point onwards the activity is self-sustaining as far as interest is concerned. Some young people, unfortunately, lack the adult backup so that they do not seek out new interests or get no support with any difficult transitions at the outset.

Advantages of Involvement in Interests

- Social interaction especially with peers but also with new groups.
- Checking out a range of abilities, learning more about themselves.
- Developing new skills: physical, social, organisational and team skills.
- Helps develop a range of secondary skills (interest in communicating, reading, writing).
- Openness to new experiences in general.
- Learning to deal with competition, success and failure.
- Increasing their vocabulary of need-satisfying activities.
- Increasing the range of activities available for different locations, weather conditions, social contexts, age-groups.
- Increasing ways to maintain physical and mental well-being.
- Offsetting boredom.
- Building a sense of achievement and helping self-esteem.

- Providing counter-balancing alternatives to the seriousness of life.
- Can give a positive motivation to life.
- May help in career development.
- An asset in curriculum vitae.

With those who reach the teen years without a constant input of interesting activities in their childhood there can be problems. The basic skill of perseverance may not be there and it may be extra hard for them to overcome the initial obstacles to really experiencing a new interest area. Teachers are well placed to help draw the attention of young people to new interests and hobbies.

Encouraging More Interests

- Use lists (or word-squares) of leisure activities in discussion.
- Display posters and notices that illustrate a good variety of activities.
- Create as much direct experience as possible of a wide range and variety of leisure pursuits, especially those that are most accessible. It is vital that the participants experience the positive side of the activity.
- Use as many sports, hobbies and pastimes as possible that incorporate many different experiences (e.g., drama, film-making).
- Involvement in fund-raising for charities and in direct charity work (e.g., "meals-on-wheels").
- Encourage people to follow one or two sports teams and constantly refer to their progress in conversation.
- Arrange competitions (but not too competitive) in a range of activities.
- Put the young people in contact with those who have a contagious interest in something.
- Organise visits to places/events with strong interest potential.

- Organise talks/videos about specific interest areas.
- Create awareness of the range of activities and events for young people in the locality.
- Create clubs for specific interests.
- Have a hobbies exhibition every two years.

Hobbies and interests have ways of enriching a child's general education. The school's active involvement in these also enhances the image of the school in the mind of the students.

Teachers, of course, also have hobbies and interests. Getting to know these can be very useful when it comes to creating clubs in the school since teachers can become the sponsors of clubs that share their interests.

The Club Fair

Unashamedly copying a tradition observed in Trinity College Dublin, we introduced the idea of a club fair to take place roughly two weeks into the first term.

This was surprisingly simple to organise since existing club members immediately saw the advantages of such an event and were keen to arrange their own participation.

A public area of the school was chosen as the venue. Each club in the school was invited to participate and the relevant teachers were given some basic guidelines.

"Your club will be allocated a table as a focus point. You as the teacher in charge of this club should supervise and manage your club's involvement in the event. Arrange to have at least two club members staffing this table throughout the event, on a rota if necessary. They should be able to promote the club, answer questions about it and take down the names of interested parties. Ideally, make your 'spot' as attractive and as informative as possible. Use photographs, posters and artefacts. Have paper and pen ready to note down names. Be prepared to have an introductory meeting for all interested students within a week of the club fair."

Normally the event was held for a full morning but different year groups were allocated specific visiting times for the event. Staff accompanying a group to the fair would be available for general stewarding of the event.

If possible an additional table could be staffed with a notice inviting ideas for new school clubs. In general students were encouraged to consider starting a new club to develop their interests.

As well as a club fair held at the beginning of the school year, individual clubs could hold "open days" during the academic year giving other students a chance to sample what the club does.

If school is a place of education and not merely an examination preparation centre then it needs to cater for the students' overall development. When a teenager gets out of bed in the morning to go to school, the more positive experiences that school represents, the more motivated will the student be to attend.

There are many other advantages in having a good club infrastructure in a school. General interests feed into the motivation for school subjects and, in many cases, lay good foundations for career planning.

Here are a few ideas for clubs that your school might not have considered:

Aviation Club: for all those interested in any aspect of flight, flying, drones, flight simulators, kites, radio communications. Such a club can inspire greater interest in physics, applied mathematics, geography.

Journalist Club: for those keen to write about any subject and contribute to an in-house news bulletin or even make contributions to local news media.

Radio Club: where a weekly news bulletin about the school and related stories is recorded and edited for "transmission" on a specific lunchtime.

Hospital Radio: the members contribute to a regular recording that is later transmitted on a local hospital's internal radio.

Heavy Metal Club: a remarkable way of bringing together kids who are generally on the margins and who tend to be left on those same margins of our society.

Write a Play Club: some of the best TV series of recent times have been put together by a team of writers and creative thinkers. This provides an ideal model for a group of students to write a short play.

Make a Film Club: similar to the above. There are many options here: learn about photography, video editing; acting; lighting; sound; make a documentary; record a school event; create a fictional film; link to a school drama club.

Environmental Awareness Club: this can help raise awareness in the school and seek ways for the school itself to improve its ways of safeguarding our environment. The group could take on a local environmental project.

Twinning Club: a group that "twins" with students in another school perhaps in a different country or language area.

Computer Programming Club: this can form around one particular language or be more general. Short courses in specific programming languages and procedures could be incorporated.

Magic Club: members can be invited to share tricks with the rest, exchange books about magic and view videos of famous magicians.

Robotics Club: this can link to the computer club or be quite separate.

Football Supporters' Club: each major team could have its own club of supporters in the school. This of course applies to every competitive sport and game in the life of the school.

Orienteering Club: an activity that combines sports interests with navigation skills.

If you still need convincing about the benefits of having many clubs in a school just think of the advantages of having the above associations even for those students who are not members. When they hear about club activities they are learning about a range of new areas they might not have known about otherwise.

Any individual club will need a meeting place and a sponsoring teacher. Some clubs will want to meet on a weekly basis but once a month might be sufficient for others. The teacher's role should be one of supporting and guiding but not controlling. The more the members can do for themselves the more they will learn.

The One-shot Club

Setting up a new club in a school can be a daunting business but the "one-shot club" bypasses all the difficulties. It can also play a very big role in helping specific students integrate into the school.

The idea is quite simple: an announcement is made on the school communication system that a meeting will be held in room X at time Y for all those interested in topic Z. A sample announcement would be, "Anybody interested in role-playing games is invited to a special meeting today in room A1 at 12.30."

What happens is that a collection of students from different year-groups arrive at the meeting room. Even if little else takes place they immediately see and meet other students who share their interest. In the following days, weeks and even years there are new bonds between students and new opportunities to share their interests. One valuable aspect of such a "club" is that it transcends age groups.

The one-shot club is something that can be arranged every so often with a selection of interests. These do not need to be activities that the students will actually practise on the school grounds. Here are some examples:

- Stamp collectors
- Role-playing games
- Kayaking
- Flight (simulators, flying, gliding)
- Model trains
- Drones
- Kites
- Animated film
- Linux
- Astronomy

- Photography
- Sailing

Where the one-shot club becomes especially useful is in helping more isolated students bond with the school. If you discover that one such student has a special interest, perhaps one that is not usual in the locality, a one-shot club can be organised to attract other students.

I would normally tell the target student of the plan and emphasise that he or she will not be a focus of attention in any way. Such a student can simply come along and observe. On one occasion I did get a surprise. The student in question was quite shy and had an unusual hobby, ideal subject matter for a one-shot club, a wonderful way to help him move out slowly and safely from the shelter of his shell! I gave him the usual guarantees that I would not draw attention to him in any way but that he would have a chance to see others with the same interest.

On the day of the club meeting I arrived in the room to find that it was already full of fellow-enthusiasts and the up-to-that-moment-in-time shy student was standing at the head of the room leading the discussion about different aspects of the hobby, finding out which areas each of those present was interested in. The jargon of the hobby in question was totally foreign to me but I could see immediately that the shy student had found a big group of people who spoke the same language.

It is not essential that such "clubs" last more than one meeting but sometimes they do flower into fully-formed groups in the school. Where I see that emerging as a possibility I encourage the students themselves to plan their club, choose a committee, approach school authorities for permission and talk to teachers about getting a suitable room and time for their activities. Normally they would also need to seek out a member of staff who will be their sponsor, one who will keep a watchful eye on their activities and give them any support they need.

Promoting Leisure Activities

The aim of the exercises that follow is to foster awareness of the vast range of leisure activities that young people might try. This is hopefully a first step to their wanting to try something new. It is important to expand their "vocabulary" of interesting activities to cover a range of possibilities: indoor, outdoor, active, relaxing.

Greater involvement broadens their horizons, strengthens social skills, builds confidence, provides temporary respite from the problems of life, offsets boredom and reduces the chances of involvement in drugs or crime. Some of the activities below are perfect short "filler" exercises to help change the rhythm of a class.

SHOW OF HANDS: The teacher says, "Hands up all those who have tried sailing?" By quickly covering about ten interest areas those students who hold up their hands can see others with the same interests. This can help group bonding. In a group exercise such as this avoid divisive interests such as asking what teams they support.

CHECKLIST: Provide each student with a list of activities including games, sports, hobbies and general interests. Ask them to rate these as "tried already", "don't know about", "would like to try". Encourage discussion of their answers.

RANKING: Provide the students with a list of activities and invite them to rank them according to any one of several characteristics (or each team could take a different characteristic): physical activity, number of participants, danger, cost, local access/availability, suitability for different ages.

CLASSIFICATION: Again using a list of activities students are asked to group them according to different categories: Sports v Games, Indoor v Outdoor, Safe v Dangerous, Free v Costly, Individual v Team, Relaxing v Energising, Games using a ball v Games requiring a net. Games needing a field.

CLUB AND LEISURE FAIR: Representatives from different clubs and leisure activities have an exhibition stand where they can demonstrate some of the equipment or activities and encourage new members to join. Ideally this should take place early in the school year and target new students but not exclusively.

ONE SHOT CLUB: Announce, for example, "All those interested in role-playing games are invited to a ten minute meeting in room X at 12.30 today". A staff member then manages the brief meeting where the main objective is that students get to know others around the school who have similar interests. This activity is particularly useful when it targets the more introverted interests as it sets up school-wide friendship networks.

POSTERS: Ask students to choose an activity, one that they have not been involved in already, and to make a poster attracting people to participate in that activity.

QUIZ: Have a quiz in any format with leisure activities as the theme or ask students to make up their own quiz about leisure activities.

EXPERIENCE: Over a certain amount of time students are asked to try out one new activity and make a short report to bring back. (This could form part of official projects or tasks.)

OUTINGS: Class groups go to try an activity together. This could be paired with other tasks: writing a report, photographic display, video recording, web page.

WORD SQUARES or CROSSWORDS: Created with leisure activities in the squares.

FEELINGS: Provide students with a list of leisure activities and ask them to identify the feelings that they think they would experience if involved in each of the activities. Each activity may be associated with one or more feelings. Or, name a feeling and ask what activities you could choose to get that feeling.

CHARADES: Individuals take turns to mime a particular leisure activity and the rest guess what it is. An alternative to miming is for the person to write a clue on the board, adding an extra clue every so often until the rest identify the activity.

ALPHABET: Taking each letter of the alphabet in turn, participants are invited to name leisure/fun activities that begin with that letter.

RATINGS: Provide a short list of leisure activities. Start with an open discussion of the benefits of participating in these. Then ask the group members to rate each of the activities (1-5) on each of these characteristics: fun potential, exercise level, good for the mind, good for getting to know people, good for learning useful skills, good for helping you relax.

SCHOOL HOBBIES EXHIBITION: This might be organised every two years. It has the advantage of including hobbies that might not normally be part of school life. For example, model train fans can put together a massive railway layout! Model aircraft or drone enthusiasts can arrange an air display in the football field! My own school, St. Malachy's College in Belfast, even had a group of rocket enthusiasts long before the days of space travel!

First Year Video

Back in 1982 the school acquired its very first video camera. It was intended more as a video player than as a recorder but I spotted a useful purpose for it in the guidance context, a use that was eventually to contribute to a new school tradition.

Part of my goal at that time was to help new students settle into the school and I could see a good role for video recording. The idea is simple: invite students to prepare a few lines about themselves, record this on video and, one week later, play the full class video back to them all. The members of any one class heard their classmates' self-descriptions twice, once during the recording and again during the playback.

This proved to be a great confidence builder and group bonding exercise all in one. Student self-descriptions ranged from routine age and hair colour contents to zany remarks such as "... and I'm trapped in a human body" or "... and I hate girls".

What started out as a group bonding and self-development exercise acquired a new significance when we decided to show the video again on those students' last day in the school, a showing that has now become an annual tradition. Indeed, the tradition now extends to class reunions where the thirty-somethings relive their first days at school with their video playing on a big screen. Eventually, as technology advanced, we were able to present each leaving student with a DVD copy of the video. Nowadays digital files can be shared more easily.

At this stage almost every teenager carries a complete photography kit in the form of a mobile phone. However, there is still room for a short formal video of the students during their first days in the new school.

- Ensure that the school has permission to make video footage of the students.
- In a previous class session invite the students to prepare a short paragraph about themselves, sharing information that would help their classmates get to know them starting with their full name.
- For recording purposes it is advantageous if a single location can be used for all the class groups. Set up the camera on a tripod and make sure there is a good microphone close to the student, preferably on a microphone stand. Good lighting is important also. Choose a simple backdrop, plain and uncluttered.
- Ensure that you have a full class group for the recording, not one that is split or combined for optional subjects otherwise the missing students can be hard to track down.
- Call out two students to demonstrate to the others what you are going to do.
- Place one student in the "shooting" position at the microphone.
- Have the other student in the "standby" position, ideally seated about 2 metres to one side of the shooting position.
- Explain that after you focus the camera you will hold up your hand. That means that everybody should be totally quiet and the student in front of the camera gets ready.
- Then you will lower your hand. That means that the student in front of the camera can start.
- When the student finishes he or she must stay in front of the camera until you say, "NEXT".
- Then the student who has recorded goes away (for example, to the right of the camera), the standby student moves in front of the camera and the next student in the group to the left moves to the standby position.
- Once the explanation/demonstration is complete you can begin.

It is frequently difficult to get people to be first and there are sometimes differing opinions in the general body about what order people should be in. It is best to clarify this at the very beginning and if the general group of students can be seated it becomes easier for the teacher to choose a shooting order (not necessarily starting at the front of the group).

Sometimes there is a student who is genuinely upset at the idea of talking in front of the camera with others present. As discreetly as you can send the person to the back of the queue and say you will deal with them later. As the shooting progresses you can keep an eye on this person. At the end you will probably find it easier to shoot this person after all the others have gone back to class. If they are still reluctant, encourage them as much as possible reminding them that in several years time they will regret not being in the video with their friends. As a last resort say it is sufficient just to say their name.

Quite often students will get giggles in front of the camera. This is part of their nervousness and it is part of who they are. I usually shoot some of this but if it goes on too long I stop the camera temporarily. Dealing with this in a relaxed matter-of-fact way is better than taking a harsh approach. A good atmosphere is vital for the entire video-shoot.

Shooting

- Follow the procedure outlined above.
- Frame the student so that you get at least head and shoulders, occasionally zooming to a head-shot to add variety to the final video.
- When you hold up your hand as a ready signal, press the button to start shooting before you lower your hand as the camera normally takes a few seconds to start rolling.
- Stop the camera shooting before saying NEXT.

At the end of a class shoot press and hold the FADE button on the camera so that the image goes blank and then shoot a few seconds of blank screen. This helps distinguish the class groups. I used to name the class groups, even put titles on the screen, but I stopped this since the video will eventually be seen by many people and some might not want others to know what class they were in. If you can manage the camera settings it can be useful to have the date as a subtitle.

About two weeks after taking all the classes do a round up of all students who missed the video and have a special shooting session for them. I allow two weeks since the absentees are often sick or away on a trip. A two week delay gets around most of these factors. Ultimately there will always be a few you will miss and it is up to you to decide how many extra shoots you can cope with.

The video should not be shown to any other classes until such times as it is shown on the day they leave school.

The Final Day

In St. Oliver's Community College that final day for students is a well-planned celebration. The morning is taken up by several assemblies arranged by the group's Year Head and school management. Lunch time is devoted to a staff-student football match. The survivors of this then re-assemble to watch the video recording. This normally takes between 60 and 90 minutes.

The final event of their formal school attendance is a party in the staff room. Staff members act as hosts and even as waiters. This is one of the most positive events in the school calendar.

Not to be outdone, students have evolved yet another tradition and they initiate their new out-of-school life by organising a social event at a local establishment and they invite staff to this.

There were a few additions I made to the video copy that was given as a gift to the school-leavers. In recent years I had taken about 5 minutes of video of their first moments in the school, shooting the new students coming through the doors wide-eyed and then taking their seats in the assembly area as the principal welcomed them to their new school. Then, on their final day, I positioned the camera strategically so that I could video them all as they flocked into the staff-room for the party. These extra two video clips formed a perfect addition to the video record of their school years.

We strive to make education a positive experience from the new students' very first encounter with the school. We do our best to make the intervening years of classes, activities and examinations as positive as possible. The students' last day of formal education with us completes this important phase in their lives and does so in an atmosphere of collaboration and celebration. A school experience like that stays in the treasured memories of life, and not just for the students!

A Student Advocate Scheme

In every school there are always a number of children, maybe 1%, who cannot be dealt with adequately by the school and its current resources. There is another slightly bigger group, maybe 5%, who are "difficult". Again, shortage of resources means that when these children are absent teachers notice the difference. Very often they interfere with the education of their classmates and, at least for a time, it is best for the class and, indeed, for the individuals concerned, if they are removed from the classroom.

In spite of how widespread this situation is very few schools have a place or process for such children within the school. At the same time these children are not only equally entitled to an education but by their behaviour they vividly demonstrate their increased need for such. These notes outline a possible mode of interaction with these children. It is not meant to be a complete solution but does create an extra support infrastructure for them.

The children to include

Although individual details may differ they tend to have a remarkable number of characteristics in common:

- forgetful of books and equipment
- frequently late, poor attendance
- scruffy, unkempt
- hyperactive, disruptive
- defiant, fearless
- impulsive, temperamental
- irresponsible
- rarely does work, homework
- angry, aggressive
- insensitive to others
- unclear speech

- sometimes promiscuous
- foul language
- scatty
- piercings, tattoos
- malnourished
- limited self-awareness
- limited sense of future/planning
- parental apathy/negativity/inadequacy
- excess freedom, street-wise
- involvement in fringe activities, drugs
- low literacy/numeracy levels
- low discomfort threshold
- rejection of teachers/adults

The practical goals of the strategy

- aim to replace what has been missing in the child's life; this can be summed up by friendliness, firmness and fairness
- communicate these characteristics with amplified clarity to the young person
- connect with the child in a positive way
- not use the relationship in any conditional way, neither reward or punishment
- attend to continuity, stability
- help the child make sense of his or her world
- provide new personnel and physical structures within the school to this end

Main components of the strategy

- to create a new professional relationship, that of "advocate" with the child operating within the school but outside the individual classroom situation
- to seek parental cooperation in this strategy rather than hope for full parental re-education (which could take longer than the student's childhood)

- to reduce suspension as this often returns the child to the roots of the problem
- to create a "time out room" or similar arrangement for re-connecting (The time-out facility is the subject of another chapter.)

Characteristics of an advocate

- not necessarily a current teacher of the child
- has a positive attitude to the child ... and to children in general
- voluntary participation in the scheme
- has good awareness of the school team and how it works
- tolerant, not easily shocked
- willing to learn new skills

The Pairing Arrangement

- advocate meets with several kids and identifies one to work with
- works with an individual not a group, always one-to-one
- has a special induction programme with the child

General duties of an advocate

- unconditional positive relationship
- ideally get to know the child before entry to the school
- brief daily contact, preferably informal
- find out about child's interests and strengths
- chat with rather than talk to
- listen to concerns
- get to know personal/social background
- act as an advocate interceding for the child in conflicts
- seek the best deal for child
- be friendly, fair and firm

- discuss the relevance of school subjects
- extra: monitor child's individual learning plan (ILP)
- extra: liaise with the child's tutor and year head
- extra: liaise with the child's parents or guardians
- extra: liaise with teachers/learning support/guidance counselling and other support staff
- extra: attend class meetings involving the child

Training for Advocates

- basic psychology of human behaviour, understanding the child
- psychology of cognitive development of the child
- psychology of the learning zone (Vygotsky's ideas)
- listening and mediation skills
- affirmation skills (avoiding punishment and praise approaches)
- role-playing skills
- practicalities of time-out room management
- anger management for teenagers
- clarification of the advocate role: defining practicalities of "professional friendship"

The advocate scheme is specifically intended to aid those children who are most likely not to survive formal education without special intervention. It also provides the teachers involved with a different experience of school giving insights into the special difficulties some students face.

Class by Class Support

Many schools use some form of "Class by class report" for students with behavioural difficulties but sometimes the purpose of this exercise is unclear. It could be part of a detailed monitoring system to check on a student's behaviour in the wake of some unacceptable conduct. Typically the student is given a sheet with spaces for a week's classes and is expected to get each teacher to write a comment and sign the sheet. A clear idea of the strategy's purpose is important or it can backfire.

The single most powerful value of such an approach is to help the student's self-awareness and for that reason I prefer to think of a "class-by-class support". At the beginning of every class the student is helped remember to focus on his or her own behaviour. For many students such self-awareness is under-developed mainly due to the lack of the cognitive ability to perceive beyond immediate experience and, for the same reason, any intervention that requires the student to plan over a week or longer is unlikely to work.

An hourly reminder such as a class by class report can begin the process of self-awareness. However, if its content is negative then there are several possible outcomes: (1) a negative comment does not teach or affirm appropriate behaviour, (2) the student will want to lose the form and (3) the student may be discouraged from trying to behave, to co-operate or even to become more self-aware. If the school requires behavioural statistics on the student the relevant data can be kept in a teacher's own class records. Where the aim is to help the student's self-awareness and ultimately his or her sense of responsibility then the following may be more appropriate ways.

Positive class-by-class report: The student has a form with a space for every teacher to comment and sign. However, only positive affirmations may be made by the teacher. This is essential. If the student has not behaved well this may be dealt with by other means but will not be recorded on the class by class report.

The student should give the form to the teacher at the start of the class, something that allows for some positive interaction at the outset. It is important that remarks are affirmations (acknowledging specific student achievements and progress such as "asked interesting questions in class", "had all materials ready") rather than general praise (such as "excellent", "good"). The student receiving such affirmations will begin to become more aware of his or her own behaviour, will have guidelines about how to continue improvement and will tend to increase the number of good reports. Inappropriate behaviour will literally be pushed out by the appropriate behaviour.

Student self-evaluation: This is similar to the Positive Class by Class Report but is kept privately by the student. The student keeps a record of his or her own behaviour. The individual student might discuss its contents with the guidance counsellor but the form will not be part of any discipline procedure and the teacher will not see it. Such a form can be a good progression from the Positive Class by Class Report as it emphasises the student's responsibility for self.

Class-by-class support: For students who have difficulty keeping to plans the teacher in consultation with the student agrees to give him or her a gentle discreet reminder at the beginning of every class. It is essential that the student perceives this as a gesture of help rather than admonishment.

The teacher could use a general greeting such as "How are things today?", any phrase or gesture provided the student knows it is part of the support plan. It is important always to use the same phrase or gesture. Initially all the student's teachers might be involved and the reminder is issued at the start of every class. As the plan progresses the number of interventions can be reduced gradually (e.g., one in morning and one in afternoon). Maintaining consultation with the student is important so that he or she sees the intervention as supportive.

Reconnecting with Returning Students

Many schools have no in-house system for dealing with seriously disruptive students and end up suspending them for a period of time. Whatever the benefits or otherwise of such a scheme it is vital that some thought be given to the time when that student returns to the school. It would be folly to assume that the child will always return with improved behaviour and attitudes. It would be equally foolish to keep doing the same thing and to expect different results.

PREPARE: Be prepared in advance for the student's re-entry, having a strategy ready for the very first point of contact. Without a plan the student is likely to get into difficulties very quickly.

RELATIONSHIP: Establish a positive relationship before anything else. Approach the student (rather than waiting for a chance meeting) and say a few friendly words. It's probably better to do this somewhere other than in front of the student's peers. When a relationship is negative the other party spends more time in defensive mode than in collaborative or creative mode.

CO-OPERATION: Tell returning students that you are prepared to work with them to help them keep their place in the course and that their co-operation is vital. Having a secret alerting system as outlined below helps communicate your co-operation. Show that your focus is on helping them rather than on trying to catch them out.

CRISIS: Tell them that if they get angry about something then you can talk about it with them when both sides have cooled down. This models good mood management.

CONTACT: At the point of entry to the class, for example as the students file past you, give the returning student a greeting that communicates the new positive approach that is now on offer. This may be no more than a smile or may be a few words of friendly chat.

ATTENTION: Particularly in the first five minutes of a class session a nod or smile in the student's direction will help strengthen the positive relationship further. Students often receive notice only when they are already disrupting the class. In the early stages it will be important to keep regular contact with the student in and out of class. Whatever the teacher pays attention to the students learn to pay attention to. If positive notice is given to a student, that person's self-awareness has the better chance of growing. Because the student's own attention-span may be limited, frequent contact is vital. After a class, especially a good one, ask, "How did that go for you?" and "What did you do that made the difference?"

CONCRETE: Strategies that involve promises or any other form of long-term plan from the student will be unlikely to be very successful in themselves. A returning student will probably need a concrete short-term approach rather than an abstract long-term one. One hour at a time!

CHOICES: A two-step alerting system will help deal with disruptive or angry behaviour. In advance you can tell the student that he or she will get two alerts about any behaviour that is disrupting others. (Initially it is probably best to focus only on what is disruptive to others. Behaviour that is unproductive or detrimental to self can become the focus at a later date.)

These alerts should be low-key, done in a way that other students are not aware of them. Equally important is that the alerts convey collaboration rather than threat. At the earliest possible time intervene in a potentially disruptive situation by discreet signalling. Agree a secret signal for this with the student beforehand. For example, the teacher might hold a single finger to her own lips as a signal.

If the behaviour continues or is repeated shortly afterwards the student is asked to do something specific that prevents further disruption. This may be to go to a separate part of the room, to go to the back of another teacher's class or to go to a special room. It may also involve a link to the school's contract system.

The idea of these steps is that the student gets an opportunity (1) to become aware of her behaviour and (2) to make a choice about it. If her disruption is obviously serious it may require a more active intervention from the outset. This may be necessary at times but there is less learning in such an intervention. A vital component of this system is the communication of a collaborative relationship with the student, not one of external control.

TOLERANCE: Some degree of tolerance will be important. At the same time, what is regarded as a level 1 behaviour from one student might be seen as a level 2 behaviour from another. Classmates may need to learn that being treated equally is not the same as being treated identically. We are all equal but we are not all the same!

CALM: At all times it is vital for the staff-member to remain calm in dealing with the student. The boy or girl will learn this more easily on seeing it modelled. Having a well-prepared strategy set up in advance makes it easier to remain calm.

It is important that the student returning after an enforced absence should get a clear message that the school wants to help that student grow in a positive way.

Time-out

This is not necessarily a physical room but is a space set aside for helping children whose behaviour has become too disruptive for the normal classroom. Teachers quite rightly claim that disruptive behaviour interferes with the rights of the majority in the class to an education. It is equally true that the disruptive child also has a right to education and educators have a responsibility to provide for such children.

There is no one solution that suits all schools and, indeed, any one school might adopt several options. What is vital to understand is that the time-out option must never be seen as a punishment. It is not detention and it is not suspension! It is a remedy, a way of helping a student develop and it is vital that this purpose is made clear to the individual.

Whatever method or methods a school adopts, it is important to speak about these to students well in advance of any incidents. In a calm and collaborative tone explain that the idea is to give the young person an opportunity to reflect on his or her situation and to return to normal class as soon as possible. It is also a way for everyone to remain friends.

It is important that the teacher who encounters the disruption should make an attempt to understand its origins. Does the student not understand what is going on in the subject? Has the person some more generalised learning problem? Are there other things going on in the student's life? Is a more varied teaching style required? Consultation with the guidance counsellor or with some other teachers of the same child may shed light on the problem. At the same time the teacher needs a strategy that can be applied immediately in the classroom.

It is easy for a teacher to become irritated by disruptive behaviour but this is less likely to overflow into anger if he or she has a well-planned intervention ready for such situations.   It is part of the teacher's professional preparation to know how to deal with all sorts of students. Here are some of the options.

Special corner of the classroom: Several sports make allowance for sending a player to the sideline for a short time to cool off. An important characteristic of this approach is that it is only for a short time, maybe 5 or 10 minutes. "Just sit over there for a wee while, Joan, and let me know when you are ready to join in again."

Outside the door of the classroom: If the disruptive behaviour relies on having an audience, it may be important to move the student out of view of that same audience. However it is vital that the teacher is able to supervise the student. Ask the student to stand or sit just outside the door but in a position where the teacher can see him or her at all times. A screened-off area within the classroom can serve the same purpose very well.

Special corner of the corridor: I know one school where the corridors have small alcoves. These have been equipped with a desk and two chairs to accommodate students who need some time outside the classroom.   A member of staff on corridor supervision keeps an eye on alcove occupants.

Special corner in a colleague's classroom: A teacher can make a prior arrangement with a colleague in a near-by classroom so that a disruptive student can be sent there for a short time.

Three-minute walk: Yet another option is to send the student on a short walk.   For example, the student could be given a specially prepared note that must be taken to the school office for a signature. It is vital that all concerned are aware that this is not a punishment.

Library desk: If a school has a supervised library then it can provide a suitable location for a time-out student, perhaps in a special corner of the area.

Special room: A spare room in the school can be set aside as a for a "time-out room". This could be supervised by someone allocated this responsibility or by staff who are otherwise off-duty and who volunteer for the task.

There are several characteristics of the time-out approach:

- It is intended to help the child develop.
- It is carried out in a spirit of calm collaboration.
- It is not punishment and is not seen as punishment.
- It is not a disciplinary matter and no long-term records of this will be kept.
- Neither is it attractive, certainly not more attractive than being in normal class.
- It is very temporary.
- The child is supervised at all times.
- Ideally, adult intervention is available to help the child reflect and learn.
- Normally the child will be given some work to do to keep in step with the class or to catch up.
- It will coincide with normal class times.
- The child will have the same breaks as others.

If the time-out approach is not working for an individual child, then the matter warrants a meeting of several teachers who know the child to discuss further steps. If time-out is well managed any further steps will be quite rare.

Further steps might include referral to the guidance counsellor, to specialist teaching, a meeting with parents, referral to external support services.

As in all cases where student behaviour is far from ideal it is important to look for the underlying reasons. Time-out options are aimed mainly at flare-ups that need to be managed for the good of all. Reasons for the young person's behaviour require some attention also. If the child is not finding class work need-satisfying, then behavioural problems are more likely. It may be that the student has fallen behind or requires a different type of approach. All factors need to be considered.

Standardised Testing

By standardised tests we are including tests that have been carefully prepared to provide reliable and valid measures of a person's achievement, ability or other personal attributes. Some of these are controlled so that only specially qualified professionals may administer them, others are more generally available.

Advantages for the Student

- Measures current level
- Gives experience of following instructions
- Gives experience of doing tests, coping with time-limits
- Gives experience of coping with difficulties
- Can measure progress
- May help identify specific abilities or difficulties

Advantages for the Centre or School

- Establishes baseline of abilities and general group level
- Quantifies need for extra resources
- Can contribute to local and national statistics for trend analysis and longer-term resource planning
- Offsets subjective impression (always present) of students
- Identifies tasks for Individual Learning Plan (usually with follow-up diagnostic testing)
- Useful for transfer information to/from other centres/schools
- Useful to establish standards of functional literacy/numeracy
- Useful to identify preventative measures in earlier education

Disadvantages

- Can confirm or foster "failure identity"
- Normative data may not be relevant, precise or up-to-date
- Inadequate floor or ceiling may reduce the value of the results
- Not always suitable for fine measurement of progress: Marie Clay the creator of the "Reading Recovery" programme said, "Standardised tests are poor measures of slow progress" (2002)
- Do not feed into Individual Learning Plans
- May not be sufficiently culture-free or may depend heavily on good literacy levels
- Can have an unreal face validity for some
- May have more value for statistics than for individual education

Issues to deal with

- Staff training in psychometrics
- Factors involved in choosing tests
- Up-to-date norms and creation of internal norms
- Age appropriateness
- Adequate floor and ceiling and appropriate range
- Use of meaningful scores
- Distinguishing purpose: baseline, diagnosis, pedagogy, achievement
- Creating the environment for testing
- Involvement of students in their own testing process
- Maintenance of positive testee attitudes towards testing

Standardised tests have positive uses but they should not be viewed as universally better than other forms of assessment. Marie Clay gave an insightful summary of these considerations:

I have come to regard normative, standardised tests as having a place in education, but only as an indirect way for teachers to obtain information about students' learning. When compared with the observation of learners at work, tests scores are mere approximations or estimates that do not provide good guidance to the teacher of how to teach a particular child. At times those scores present results stripped of the very information that is required for designing or evaluating sound instruction for individual learners. Standardised tests need to be supplemented at the classroom level with systematic observations of children who are in the act of responding to instruction, observations that are reliable enough to compare one child with another or one child on two different occasions. (2002)

Some measuring instruments, such as Problem Checklists, really should not be standardised at all (except for research purposes) since the responses are so subjective. Their great value is in helping young people identify problem areas rather than in quantifying the problems, a task best left to a counselling session.

Another use of almost all tests, even those of doubtful validity, is as a way to stimulate discussion.

Alternative Homework

There are several problems associated with homework: the students do not like it, everyone gets the same, it is sometimes given out without adequate planning, sometimes it is given as a punishment, the teacher needs to follow it up promptly and thoroughly. Another quite serious problem is that teachers give homework in isolation without taking into consideration what other teachers are doing. The end result can be very stressful for students.

The chief purposes of homework should be to "learn by doing", to allow an independent attempt by the student to process the work presented in class and to provide a chance for the student to assimilate the material. To these ends homework will give a chance for personal familiarity with the material, practice and testing what is known or not.

Unfortunately most students receive the same homework tasks and this goes against the aim of the individual assimilation of material. In homework relating to the Pythagoras Theorem in mathematics, for example, one student may need to revise the theorem itself, another may need revision of squares and square roots whilst yet another may benefit from lots of practice in basic calculations. For all students to do the same ten or so questions for homework will mean boredom for those who are ahead and confusion for those who are struggling.

This chapter offers several alternatives to traditional homework and I believe it would be worthwhile for a teacher to try out each approach at least once.

DIY Homework

This is more appropriate for older students. Once a week the student is asked to design and do his or her own homework. As evidence that this work has been done there will be a standard expectation of output, for example, one page of written material. The student will be asked to write out an aim for the homework, for example, to master the calculations involved in applying Pythagoras. The student is free to seek the teacher's advice about what aim to choose.

In the next class the students work in pairs. Each explains to his or her partner what was done in the homework. The second student learns as much as possible about this from the first and they check the work together. After say ten minutes they reverse roles and check the other student's homework. In the event of any difficulty the teacher may be called. At the end of the work in pairs there is a chance for a general question time with queries addressed mainly but not exclusively to the teacher.

The aim of this approach is to create homework space tailored to the needs of each student, to encourage initiative for individual learning, to foster social and caring skills through collaborative work in class, to reframe the role of the teacher as a helper in the learning process.

Team Homework

Encourage several students to work together on the homework. Ideally suggest different roles for each team member in advance so that no one team member ends up doing all the work. The real world works in teams and this approach can add excitement and realism to what is normally a rather solitary activity.

Here I have a confession to make! As a boarder at school in Belfast I was often low on pocket money. A fellow boarder and I came up with a grand money-making scheme based on team homework. Together we worked on the weekly Latin translation homework, then made multiple carbon-copies and sold the finished result to day-boys for six-pence each! We actually learned a lot of Latin and, as an adult, my friend went on to develop new economic theories ... but not about Latin!

The Flipped Learning Model

This is an idea that has been around for some time but has more recently been revived and updated. It is certainly worth a try and might be used on an occasional basis as a change from more traditional homework formats.

The normal role of homework is to extend the work done in class and to serve as a revision, assimilation and evaluation exercise. At the next class the assignments are corrected together with follow-up clarifications.

Flipped learning more or less reverses this format. For example, a history class might be asked to watch a short video from the Internet at home, one that lasts about 15 minutes and dealing with a specific topic. Students can watch the recording as often as they wish and then make a short summary of what they have learned and add one question to bring to the teacher next day.

In the next class the video and summaries are discussed and questions are dealt with. One advantage over traditional homework is that the student is unlikely to become stuck or to engage in a series of frustrating items if dealing with material that was not learned adequately in the first place. Another advantage is that the video can be paused and replayed as often as the student deems necessary. Perhaps the biggest advantage of all is that the young person is learning about learning itself. The format is also more in keeping with new technological developments.

A Presentation Project

Rather than answer questions or write an essay, invite students to do a presentation, one they can deliver in the class in, say, 10 minutes. Obviously this approach would not work if applied to the whole class group at the same time. One way to deal with this is to provide it as an option, one that requires prior consultation with the teacher. The student could work alone or as part of a team. The presentation could be spoken, accompanied by a slide show, or could be a short video made by the students themselves. An interesting rule to add to this homework is that the students must enjoy it!

One day many years ago I entered a class where I had assigned a short homework the previous week. Two young ladies in the back row were quite upset and when I enquired about this they protested that two boys in the class had actually enjoyed their homework! I was amazed at such a protest but also very curious about how the boys had managed to enjoy the task. On quizzing them I discovered that they had teamed together and had explored the topic using the only computer encyclopaedia available at that time. They were justifiably proud of the end result and I was happy at their initiative.

A Practical Project

Rather than a pencil and paper homework, students could be assigned a project that requires some field work or an experiment. Examples: a short survey of local opinions about sports amenities in the area; a study of noise levels in the local town centre using a smart phone app; measure the heights of local trees and telegraph poles using trigonometry; do a drawing or painting of a local public building.

Recorded Homework

Some students are daunted by the prospect of writing and all students benefit from spoken exercises. Arrange a homework where the responses are to be recorded. The resulting files can be emailed to the teacher. Several years ago an enterprising programmer from Drogheda created a system for students to answer recorded questions in the Irish language using their mobile phones.

No Homework

Yet another approach is to have a short weekly progress test in your subject. Provided that the overall class average score increases by a pre-determined amount each week there will be no homework given. However, students are encouraged to do whatever study they need to help push the average up and they may request ideas from the teacher. If averages remain the same for more than two weeks or if they fall by a predetermined amount even in one week then mandatory homework for all is reintroduced until the averages rise again.

Once, when suggesting the "no homework if grades improved" approach to a group of teachers, one member of the audience voiced his doubts. He believed that some students might cheat. I was puzzled about how students might do this and asked the teacher to explain the cheating. "Well," he explained, "they might do extra study at home!" I suspect he had a wry sense of humour!

A Guidance Committee

The concept of a Guidance Committee was something I created in the early nineties and maintained for the remainder of my guidance counselling career. In those early days a priority was how to administer the growing library of information brochures about careers and courses that was emanating from further education centres. Nowadays practically everything is available on the Internet so the nature and duties of the committee would change.

The original aim was to invite a group of volunteers from non-examination classes in the senior section of the school. The resulting committee would operate from the guidance office at lunch-times. Although the focus of the committee was on supplying a service to their fellow-students there were other important advantages.

- At the outset they had the experience of applying for a position, something that would help them understand career and course applications later.
- Generally these students became extra-familiar with the world of careers and with the services of the guidance counselling department. This was information they could share with their class-mates at other times of the day.
- They also gained experience in organising trips and events. They realised how beneficial their committee experience would be on their CVs.

Managing a Guidance Committee

- Inform the students by visiting classes and inviting volunteers very early in the school-year. (Non-examination senior students are ideal.)
- Each volunteer would be given an application form to complete and obtain recommendations

from two teachers. This form listed the duties of the committee.

- The resulting group would meet and a duty roster would be agreed.
- Each day those on duty would staff the guidance office.
- The members of the Guidance Committee would also be invited to act as stewards at career events.
- At the end of the school year it became a tradition to invite the committee to a lunch outside the school together with the guidance counsellors.
- Also at the end of the school-year each member of the committee was given a certificate to testify to their work and responsibility as a member of the committee.

Sample Application Form

DUTIES OF GUIDANCE COMMITTEE MEMBERS

- Be available for at least 30 minutes twice a week during lunch-times for duty in the Guidance Office.
- Attend regularly and sign in using a special committee book.
- Administer the Career Lending Library.
- Prepare a Career Display for students.
- Take names and reservations for different career events.
- Sort and maintain Guidance brochures.
- Put up and maintain Guidance Notices.
- Attend meetings of the Guidance Committee.

Why I want to join the committee:

I am available for the above duties.

SIGNED: _____ DATE: _____

RECOMMENDATIONS
to be obtained from two teachers

I fully recommend this student for a position of responsibility in the Guidance Committee.

TEACHER SIGNATURE: _____

TEACHER SIGNATURE: _____

THE APPLICANT SHOULD RETURN THIS FORM TO A GUIDANCE COUNSELLOR

New Duties

At the present time some additional duties might be added to align with the world of information technology.

- Helping students learn how to do Internet searches for career and course information.
- Help students put together a curriculum vitae for further input from the guidance counsellor.
- Help students re-evaluate their social media inputs from the viewpoint of possible employers who increasingly check out this aspect of job applicants.

My evaluation of this scheme after many years using it is very positive. Young people welcome having special roles in school life and they can learn so much from it. One special task the guidance committee did particularly well was that of handling reservations for career events and trips.

If an event, say a trip to a university open day, had a cost in order to pay for the bus, no bookings were taken without having payment in advance. On paying, the student was given a "ticket" which served the dual purposes of being a receipt and also a reminder of the date and time of the bus. A list of paid-up students was also kept by the committee member.

The ticket issued also had another useful purpose when more than one bus was involved. Tickets were issued for each bus separately. For example, Bus A had "BUS A" marked on the ticket. Students naturally wanted to travel with pals and the solution was simple: either get the tickets for the same bus together or swop tickets with someone on the desired bus. This arrangement avoided all sorts of last minute rushes for the bus of their dreams on the day of the event,

Members of the guidance committee often handled considerable sums of money in these reservations. The resulting responsibility was always carried in a mature and meticulously accurate way.

Alternatives to Punishment

In every aspect of our lives we use whatever we think will work and, wisely, will not readily move to another strategy unless we believe it will work better. In education we need to ask constantly: "What is the purpose of what we do in the classroom?" When there is a problem we need to ask, "What strategy will work best to serve the purpose of education?"

If the aim of our work in the classroom is control then punitive methods certainly give the impression of working (although it is established that they only work in the short-term and, at best, generate temporary compliance). If the aim is the education and development of our students then we need to attend to research that reveals that punishment and even some types of praise can be counter-productive. If the strategies we are using now are in fact harmful we need to consider alternatives.

The Problems with Punishment

- It distorts and damages the relationship between teacher and student.
- It teaches that "power over" is the way. "Might is right!"
- It teaches external control instead of collaboration.
- It is damaging to the student's sense of own control and self-esteem.
- It requires constant policing or record-keeping.
- It encourages low quality, "enough to get by".
- It is more "feel bad" than "feel good" and research is showing that good feelings are vital for learning just as all threat or fear is harmful to learning.
- Punishment does not teach what to do; it focuses on what not to do.
- The content of punishment acquires a negative label: For example, "Do your Maths homework twice

for tomorrow" sends out the following signals - Homework is bad enough to be a punishment; Maths is bad enough to be used as punishment; I am a punisher!

The Problem with Seeking Excuses

- Encourages evasion of responsibility by blaming others or a situation.
- De-emphasises the importance of getting the job done.
- Wastes time that could be used in planning how to complete the task.
- Can damage the relationship.
- Encourages exaggerations and fibs.

Alternatives

- Think, "How would I want to be treated in the same situation?"
- Think, "How can I deal with this so that the student grows?"
- Use logical consequences. "You have not done the homework. When are you going to do it and give it to me?" "You are ten minutes late, how do you intend to catch up?" or "Use ten minutes at lunch-time to learn what you missed." This contrasts with arbitrary punishment which is in no way connected with the problem. Do not use logical consequences if they are harmful!
- Ask the student for his or her opinion about what they will do to rectify the situation. Do this in a collaborative way, not a threatening way.
- Give choices. "You can do the missing work now, you can bring it to me at two o'clock. If you have another suggestion I will consider it." Show that you are working *with them* not *over* or *against* them.
- Anticipate and help students deal with problems in advance. "Sean, you sometimes forget to do your

homework. What can you do right now to help you remember?" Don't forget that they weren't born with planning skills.

- Use a secret signal alerting system. "Joe, next time I see you beginning to get restless I will ask you what time it is. OK?" "Mary, I'll lift your journal and have a look at it each time I see you getting chatty."
- Use a two-step approach. "Joe, I am prepared to give you the secret signal once; the second time I will ask you to move to the back corner." This gives the student an opportunity to learn and to choose. It also shows that the teacher's priority is in helping the student improve not in catching him or her out.
- Ask for an "action replay". "Mary, you made a lot of noise when you moved that chair. Could you show me how you can move it without noise?"
- State how you feel: "I am disappointed that you should have made so much noise when I attended to the person at the door."
- Be sensitive to reasons (not excuses) for the behaviour. The student may find the work too difficult, too easy, pointless. The student may be unwell, have problems that affect concentration, have hearing or sight problems.
- Focus on positive action, planning. "You have said something very offensive to Mary. What do you intend doing about it?" Be available to help with the planning.
- Be alert to students who have turned over a new leaf.
- Never stop beneficial activities (sports participation) as punishment.
- When students need to be removed from the classroom or the school ensure that return depends on the student having a new plan.
- Don't shout. Do not be an adult who shouts at children!

- Never force apologies. You can suggest them and help formulate them but a compulsory apology is rarely sincere.
- Deliberately watch for improvement in particular students and affirm this early in a given class period.
- A few friendly words with problematic students at the class-room door as they enter is invaluable.

I came across an American saying that pointed out that the best way to show that a stick is crooked is not to argue about it or spend time denouncing it but to lay a straight stick alongside it.

In a school in Idaho Alfie Kohn saw the following words on a poster: The beatings will continue until morale improves.

The Fresh Start Approach

In the very next class you have there could well be a few students whom you expect to threaten the smooth running of the class. But let's suppose that one of them had a really good chat with someone yesterday. It may have been the principal, a guidance counsellor, a parent or even a concerned friend. This student has now decided it is time to change, time to knuckle down, pay attention and do some work.

The trouble is that you as the teacher know nothing of this intention and so when noise comes from that corner of the room it makes sense to round up the usual suspects. The individual who is full of good intentions to turn over a new leaf will see this as very unfair and the result can be devastating. In fact students usually need a lot of teachers' help if they are to get out of the negative cycle of disruption -> correction -> bad feeling -> more disruption.

How Teachers might learn about the Fresh Start

- Principals or Year Heads can tell teachers as soon as possible when a student has decided to improve his or her behaviour.
- Guidance counsellors or others in positions of confidentiality can obtain the student's permission to let teachers know about the change.
- Students themselves can be encouraged to have a quiet word with each teacher.
- A form can be used (must be totally voluntary for the student) where the student can indicate to the teacher what behaviours he or she is trying to change.
- Teachers can be on the alert for signs of a change.

What Teachers Can Do

- Develop a "fresh start" mentality and use it often.
- Frequently advertise the fact to your classes that a "fresh start" is always possible and that, if students tell you they want to change, you will give them as much help as possible. (This will include a bit of leeway as well.)
- When such students are identified to you use messages of positive support. Any hint of cynicism or even surprise can throw cold water on their good intentions.
- Understand that their intentions to change may not be matched by their ability to change. They have old habits to remove; they have new skills to learn; they will need your help.
- Help them identify what they need to do and spell out the details. Usually it is best to focus on only one or two items at a time.
- Keep plans for change simple and with a high expectation of success.
- Use plans that are positive. Planning not to do something or planning to stop something is nowhere as effective as planning to do or begin something.
- Target these students prior to class entry and have a brief friendly word with them.
- Any hint of impatience or raised voices can cause major setbacks for a fresh start process.
- When students do improve (even if this is not totally intentional on their part) give due acknowledgement. Use affirmation rather than praise (e.g., "I notice you have all your books here today" rather than "You are behaving very well today"). Affirmation identifies specific behaviours; praise tends to be general and may appear condescending.
- Draw attention to changes and to their own effort: "I notice you seem to be getting on much better in

recent times? What are you doing differently?"
Help increase their self-awareness.
- Be sensitive to the fact that even small improvements can be a big achievement for them.
- Liaise with the guidance counsellor, year head or others who may have valuable information about the student as well as ideas of how best to help the student make positive changes.
- Don't forget to send a message home about how well the student is doing.

The Fresh Start Plan

The forms described below are designed to be part of the guidance counsellor's resources.   Under no circumstances should these forms become a part of a discipline system nor should their use ever be made obligatory.

AIMS: The main purpose of the form is to help students convey to some or all of their teachers that they are attempting to change their in-school behaviour for the better. This is intended to counter the possible effects of a well-established bad reputation in the school or with specific teachers.   There is an accompanying message about "Fresh Start" and this could be circulated to staff in advance of using any Fresh Start forms.

Use of the form:

1. Ideally it should be duplicated on coloured paper but having a very different colour from those used by any discipline documentation within the school.
2. It should be offered to a student, not made compulsory.
3. The purpose of the form should be explained clearly to the student.
4. Read through the contents of the form and then ask the student if she or he wants to use it.

5. Ask if the student wants more than one copy (for more than one teacher).
6. Help the student fill in the first part "What I myself think I need to change", encouraging them to be precise and positive in their descriptions.
7. Check that the proposed changes have a high possibility of success.
8. Generally it is not a good idea to have more than two items.
9. Ask the student which teachers he or she intends showing the form to.
10. Go over the details of when the student will meet the teacher, what he or she will say.

In some cases teachers choose to return the completed form to the Guidance counsellor directly; in others they return the form to the student. When the student meets with you again help him or her process the teachers' comments. This may entail converting general instructions into specific behavioural plans. In subsequent sessions monitor the progress in both the student's proposals and the teacher's recommendations.

The Fresh Start Form

Student Name: _____ Class: _____

- I want to do better at school.
- I would like to ask for your help in doing this.
- Please suggest one or two things I could do to improve.
- I will show this to my guidance counsellor who will help me work out a plan of action.

What I myself think I need to change:

Student's Signature:

Teacher's Suggestions:

Teacher's Signature:

Message to the teacher from the guidance counsellor

This form is intended to be given to teachers chosen by the student and is aimed at helping the student overcome any deterioration in school-work or behaviour in the past. It is not a report form in the normal sense and is not disciplinary in nature. Its use is chosen freely by the young person. If a student shows this form to a teacher it is an indication that he or she wishes to improve. Any suggestions you offer should aim at helping this student plan and carry out new behaviours. Keeping the suggestions to a few that are precise, positive and possible tends to give better guarantees of success.
[END OF FORM]

The Student Self-Evaluation Form

AIMS: This is designed to help students monitor their own behaviour. The idea is that monitoring behaviour helps a person change it in the planned direction. It also increases self-awareness. Perhaps the most important advantage of this form is that it places the evaluation where it is needed most and works best, that is, in the hands of the student.

Use of the form:

1. Ideally it should be duplicated on coloured paper but using a very different colour from those used by any discipline material in use within the school.
2. It should be offered to a student, not made compulsory.
3. The purpose of the form should be explained clearly to the student.

4. Read through the contents of the form and then ask the student if she or he wants to use it.
5. Emphasise that it is for the student's own use; no adult signature or monitoring is required.
6. The student could mark the form at quiet moments, maybe even at the end of each day.
7. Encourage students to use their own marking scheme. It could be a tick for behavioural targets achieved, an "x" for a class period that did not go according to plan.
8. Model the form's use by helping the student process the last few class periods on the form.
9. Whether the student shows this to you at the next session depends on the student's own choice.

The Student's Responsibility

It is vital to distinguish between acknowledgment of the student's responsibility for his or her own life and blaming the student for his or her behaviour. Compare these two approaches, each focusing on the student's own responsibility but in quite different ways:

• You want to be punctual for class and I will do anything I can to help you achieve your goal.

• It is up to you and you alone to be punctual. You cannot blame anybody else if you are late!

The second approach is wielding the student's responsibility, using it as a weapon. The first approach gently acknowledges the same responsibility but uses words that are in no way attempting to control the young person. There is a world of difference between these two strategies. Where the focus is on controlling the student's behaviour there may well be a positive response in terms of punctuality but the losses in the relationship can have a heavy price elsewhere.

Both the Fresh Start Form and the Student Self-evaluation Form are examples of an approach based on internal control, on helping students take better control of their own life.

Student Stress

Most books and information dealing with stress focus on the physiological symptoms associated with it. They also tend to treat stress as if it were some terrible foreign invader of our little world of psychological peace and happiness. The advice offered tends to be about relaxation, about taking deep breaths or a walk in the woods. Such recommendations are fine but quite incomplete and at times off-target.

From the perspective of Choice Theory psychology (from Dr. William Glasser) all feelings are signals. They are not illnesses or disorders but highly orderly systems to alert us to the need for action. Unless we heed our signals and then address the root causes of our stress, minimising the symptoms will be counter-productive. It is akin to searching for ways to silence a ringing fire alarm instead of heeding the signal to track down and extinguish the fire that triggered it. Whether we try to silence our stress signals with relaxation exercises or with any type of drug, the stress will continue unless we address its root cause.

Stress is a set of feelings and physiological changes that arise from prolonged frustration of our basic needs. As such, stress is a red alert, telling us that something is amiss. We need to focus our attention on identifying and fixing the underlying frustration.

Anxiety is another signal, one that warns us that somehow we are facing a situation where we do not have all the preparation or skills to deal with it. It is a very useful warning that we are getting out of our depth. A big difference between anxiety and stress is that the latter has a longer life. The frustration has lasted longer and this suggests that the individual has been unable to seek or find solutions to that frustration.

Those who have not developed the habit of taking action on such feeling signals are destined to have the alarm bells continue. They become constant worriers and this will at times escalate into panic. Unattended to stress will gradually wear a person down and may give rise to serious health problems.

In young people, the causes of frustration can be many. The primary solution to stress is to identify the area or areas of frustration and to take remedial action by acquiring the information and/or skills necessary to deal with it. An important resource they need to be aware of is that of talking to someone to seek help.

When times get tough, it's time to talk!

This message becomes extra important for those in the throes of depression or considering suicide.

Crisis intervention is important and young people need to know who is available to help. Equally important is prevention by offering young people information and skills to deal with life situations.

If we help address the most typical sources of frustration in their lives, we are helping them reduce stress and anxiety. On the one hand people need to understand the nature of stress and its powerful signalling value and, on the other, they need to have access to ways of resolving their frustrations. What follows are some examples of areas to focus on for young people. For a different audience, of adults for example, other topics might be relevant such as finance, child-rearing. In all cases it is a question of identifying the areas of possible frustration and then taking steps to learn how to deal with them.

Talking: at least once in every school term the guidance counsellor or a delegated teacher could focus on the message "When times get tough, it's time to talk!" It's not enough simply to state such a message. Invite the young people to consider who they would talk to in an emergency. Invite them to identify someone privately in their own minds. Help them by listing possible allies: parents, uncles or aunts, neighbours, grandparents, a teacher, a member of the clergy, a friend of the family, the guidance counsellor or a close friend. This is an incredibly important message and should be mentioned and even published everywhere that suicide is discussed.

Sensitive Issues: related to the previous idea of talking is that of issues that many find it difficult to discuss. A guidance counsellor can draw attention to these in a classroom setting and, by the way the topics are broached, the young people can see that the counsellor will give them a sympathetic ear. Some examples are: gender identity, suicidal thoughts, self-harm, bed-wetting, scruples, being "normal". It is one of the big advantages of guidance counselling that the counsellor is able to advertise his or her approach to potential clients via classroom contact.

Relationships: many of our stresses and worries come from our relationships. Break ups, conflicts, misunderstandings, poor communication, possessiveness, controlling, criticism, bullying are all relationship problems. Our teenagers are in a phase of developing lots of new relationships and they benefit greatly from guidance sessions about relationships and associated issues.

Time management, planning and decision-making: these are all skills that are vital to a healthy psychological life and training in these areas should be built into the school curriculum.

Learning skills and examination skills: again these are important and benefit from general advice from the guidance counsellor combined with more specific advice from each subject teacher.

Sleep management: young people very often neglect their sleep patterns and benefit from information about the importance of getting enough, of maintaining a regular pattern, of the effects of drugs on sleep.

A balanced life: neglecting any of our basic needs (love and belonging, freedom, power, fun and survival) can lead to stress. Young people need to learn about the importance of a balanced life and about the role of their basic needs. Equipping young people for life includes enriching their vocabulary of ways of meeting each and all of their basic needs. Education about careers, relationships, leisure and healthy living all contribute to this.

Basic psychology: people need to understand their own feelings and the signals they carry. They need to learn about how to achieve and maintain personal well-being, so-called "mental health". Books such as "In The Driving Seat" offer group activities for a course on personal well-being.

Science: This is not simply about the "sciences" of physics, chemistry and so on. The science that we all need is about learning how to process information, how to live more effectively in harmony with our environment, how to judge our own behaviour as objectively as possible. Prejudicial thinking, superstitions and flawed logic are all signs that scientific thinking has been lacking and are recipes for frustration.

Feelings of stress are very important signals to us about how we are managing our lives. If we focus excessively on the signal and look for ways of reducing it without attending to the underlying frustration, the stress will re-emerge later. Even for a common pain such as a headache, it is good for young people to learn to examine this as a signal that something is wrong. It could be a sign of lack of sleep, of being in a smoky atmosphere and, of course, it could be indicative of some health issue. Taking a tablet for a pain or doing relaxation exercises for stress are not in themselves dealing with the underlying causes though they may be beneficial for short-term relief.

Finally, it is worth reflecting that without the physical feelings of pain and the psychological feelings of anxiety, stress and depression we could really mess up our lives. Similarly if we ignore, misinterpret or mistreat these strong signals then they are likely to continue and even worsen. If education is a preparation for life then it must include some guidance about how to deal with life's difficulties and crises.

Encouraging Peer Friendships

Students who do not relate well to their peers can become increasingly at risk as they grow older. Sometimes these young people do in fact relate very well to adults and this can disguise their inadequacies with their own age group.

Very often these students are so well-behaved that they escape the notice of adults and any difficulties they encounter can very easily accumulate without solution. When a student is not relating well to others there are some things that school staff can do to help.

A Special Job

One such intervention is to create a "job" tailored to the young person's needs.

Identify potential friends for the job.

- Ideally these should be in the same form class
- they should be caring and responsible
- they should have a similar interaction style to the target student, normally quiet
- they should have similar interests if possible

Choose an appropriate "job"

- the task should be one that requires interdependence (e.g., carrying a table)
- it should necessitate some interaction (e.g., planning how to get through the doorway)
- call them together discreetly to do the job
- they should not receive too many instructions so that they need to work out some of the details themselves
- give them time alone to plan and do the job

Help them bond at the outset:

- chat with each of them in advance of the "job"
- give them the introductory instructions
- ask each about their interests, where they are from
- draw out any topic that you know will interest all of them
- help create a base for further conversation between them
- gently teasing them may help them bond (e.g. if all are Manchester United supporters)

After the task:

- when they finish ask for a brief report from both of them
- if they have worked well as a team acknowledge this
- evaluate how useful the task was in helping the target student start networking
- if it did not go well use the lessons learned to plan a different team-mate or approach next time
- be prepared to call the two together for another job in the near future to help consolidate the bonding process (only if they got on reasonably well)

Existing Structures

Sometimes there are existing structures within a school where quiet students can group together without requiring strong social skills to begin with. For example, a school shop may need a roster of helpers and several quiet students could be given the same slot. Joining a choir is often quite safe for very quiet students but involvement in drama (on stage or off) can sometimes surprise. I recall several students who blossomed socially and almost miraculously after they joined a school drama activity.

Informal Chat

It is also possible to chat informally with a small group in the corridor. For example, on seeing an isolated student you could call a few other quiet students and that person together to ask their opinion about something topical. Ideally choose a topic that will be a strength for the isolated student.

One-Shot Club

This is another very powerful and quite simple approach explained in fuller detail elsewhere in this book. A meeting is called of students with a particular interest, the interest being one that is important for the shy student.

Praising without Harming

We congratulate ourselves and rightly so for having left physical coercion far behind us in education. Nowadays we concentrate on praising and rewarding children for what they do well … but in recent times research has been casting doubts over certain aspects of this approach!

Are we doing harm even when we praise? American educator Alfie Kohn claims that **coercion** encourages kids to become liars, lawyers or rebels. ("I didn't do it." "That's not what the rule says!" "I don't care what you say!") He claims that **punishment** does the same. The surprise is that he claims the same outcomes for **praise**! In fact he says that coercion, punishment and praise (or rewards) all foster temporary compliance (except obviously in those who rebel against it) instead of longer lasting benefits. He adds that all three damage the teacher-pupil relationship, teach that power over others is good and all three require intensive monitoring. In his book "Beyond Discipline" Kohn quotes lots of research supporting his indictment of praise, punishment and coercion. We need to take a closer look at "praise" and its effects.

Affirmation: Canadian educator Diane Gossen quotes the example of a teacher who praises the child's drawing "and the beautiful flower pattern around the edges". Result: more flower patterns around the edges for a long time to come and, a more subtle mental shift, more looking to the teacher and others for approval of his or her work. Compliance, conformity and external control are hardly the goals we would set for the education of children! The alternative, Diane suggests, is to affirm the child and give lots of attention: "Where did you get the idea for this? What are you going to draw next? Can we display it on the wall?" This does not intrude on the child's own inner control; instead it encourages thinking and creativity. It gives attention rather than evaluation and enhances rather than damages the relationship.

Precision: Faber and Mazlish, authors of "How to Talk So Kids Can Learn" recommend being precise in our affirmations. Instead of vague praise such as "Your work is fantastic!" we might say, "I notice how you spaced out your work clearly and did very neat diagrams." In other words we describe what we observe instead of making vague general statements. We don't even have to say it was good or great! The student becomes more aware of what they are doing and develops an internal valuing system. Affirmation makes better educational sense from all angles.

Positive: There is yet another advantage. Affirmation is the perfect replacement for the damaging practice of criticism. Criticism (even so-called "constructive criticism") is negative, evaluative and external. By saying what a person is doing "wrong" does not point clearly to what the person might do instead, it can harm the relationship and it may even lead to the person losing interest in the subject. Instead of "You got 15 of the 20 words wrong!", (criticism) we might say, "I see you got 5 words spelled perfectly and you have written another 10 words exactly as they sound." The student receives positive attention and will be all the more encouraged to continue to improve his or her work.

By creating this collaborative working relationship with the student it becomes easier to say, "I'm not sure what happened to the other 5 words! Do you want some help in learning how to spell all the words perfectly?" (And do not forget that the English language is a speller's nightmare!)

Talent versus Effort: There is research that points to the potential for harm if we do not refine our notion of "praise". In Columbia University, USA, psychologist Carol Dweck studied the effects of different types of praise in a dozen New York schools. After giving them a series of puzzles some kids were told, "You must be smart at this" while others were told, "You must have worked really hard". Later the same children were offered the choice of an easier test or a harder test. Of those praised earlier for their effort 90% chose the harder test. A majority of those praised for their intelligence chose the easy test.

This and even more fascinating research is reported in *How Not to Talk to Your Kids: The Inverse Power of Praise*" by Po Bronson. The author believes that those praised for being "clever" become afraid to take on anything that might undermine that reputation while those praised for **effort** get even more confident about what they can change through hard work. The affirmation approach mentioned earlier, by describing details, is more likely to emphasise effort than some vague intelligent force.

Putting These Ideas into Practice: Affirmation does not take longer than general praise or criticism. It does not even mean extra work but it does require a mental shift in the way we deal with our students. One way to achieve the mental shift is to read through these notes (or at least the summary suggestions below) once a day for about a week. Discuss the ideas with colleagues and compare notes on the approach.

- Start paying more **attention** to what students have done rather than what they have done poorly or not at all.
- Simply **describe** the positive details of what you see instead of evaluating or praising in a general way.
- Create opportunities for all students to **display** their work in the classroom or around the school.
- Invite students to tell you what they think of their work, what they would like to do next and how you

can help them in this process. (That is, constantly encourage them to use **self-evaluation** instead of applying your external evaluation to them.)

- When we identify the "top" students, first, second and third, the other 27 students in the class become "also-rans"; that's 90%! By **affirming everyone** we could have 100% involvement.
- We need to create an **atmosphere of growth**, where students know it is good and possible to move from 10% to 20%. To achieve this we need to acknowledge the 10% and 20% levels, not just the high-fliers.
- At the same time we need to eliminate the notion that a "pass" (grade C or D) is our goal. If our students want to get **100%** we will help them get it! At the very least we aim for competence, usually an A or B grade.
- Instead of "failure", think and say, "**not ready yet**".
- When you catch yourself praising or criticising **recall** the above alternatives.

This book is about education but many of these ideas apply in personal relationships of any type. Eliminate criticism in your most important relationships and you can transform them in a very positive direction.

Choice Theory Psychology

Choice Theory has been mentioned in several places in this book and underpins many of the approaches described. It is time to take a closer look.

In the early sixties Dr. William Glasser developed his approach to therapy that he called "Reality Therapy" and published in a book of the same name in 1965.

It was based very much on the individual's control of his or her own life, on personal responsibility, a control that could only influence the present and future. Those who learned this approach from what was then the Institute for Reality Therapy (now "William Glasser International") soon found that these ideas had a personal meaning. Reality Therapy was not simply a set of techniques that a counsellor applied to clients, it provided a guide to personal well-being as well. In fact, you could not really help others with Reality Therapy unless you applied the ideas to your own life.

In the nineteen eighties Glasser studied the writings of William Powers who in turn had borrowed concepts from the world of engineering about how servo-mechanisms worked. Powers' "Control Theory" helped clarify just how we processed our perceptions. In the following decade Glasser found the idea of Edwards Deming very enlightening regarding the notion of quality. These new ideas combined with his basic understanding of Reality Therapy led to the formulation of a new set of principles, "Choice Theory". In the book of that name published in 1998 Glasser called it a "new psychology of personal freedom".

It soon became clear that the reason Reality Therapy could have as much meaning for the counsellor as for the client was that it embodied this psychology. Choice Theory, the foundation of Reality Therapy, was not simply a set of counselling principles but a more general explanation of human behaviour and human happiness. It was a psychology.

Choice Theory psychology has great relevance to the work of educators for several reasons: it explains how effective relationships work; it offers a plan for personal well-being ("mental health"); it guides the counselling process. It also offers ideas about how we might influence others without attempting to control them. It is time to look at its major concepts.

At the heart of Choice Theory is the idea that the only behaviour you can control is your own. Consequently you cannot control others and they cannot control you. However we tend to live our lives thinking we can control others and believing that others can control us. We blame our problems on our inability to influence others and on their apparent ability to influence us. "I keep telling my son to tidy his room and he doesn't do it!" "The government drives me mad!" Glasser refers to this as the psychology of external control and it is the total opposite of his own internal control psychology, "Choice Theory".

The reason we are the controllers of our own behaviour is that our motivation is internal. We are driven by basic needs that in turn lead us to create our "quality world", each individual's personal collection of apparently need-satisfying people, things, places and values. It is these pictures in our quality worlds that drive our behaviour on a moment-by-moment basis. These are the situations and things that we work hard to achieve. Although others might influence us all they can do is give us information. We are "influenced" if what we see appeals to our quality worlds and we choose to act on that information.

Why does a child constantly disturb a class? Why do people smoke when they know the terrible health risks associated with it? Why does someone become obsessive about hand-washing? Why do people cross their legs? Why do people answer the telephone?

From a Choice Theory viewpoint all these people are choosing behaviours that they believe (not necessarily in a very conscious way) to be meeting their needs. If something else was more need-satisfying in that moment they would choose that something else. It would follow that anyone who wishes to help that individual should find a way to offer the person alternative and more effective ways of meeting the same needs. Tackling the presenting behaviours is unlikely to be very beneficial. Stopping people from using the only solution they know can be counter-productive.

In counselling, the Reality Therapy practitioner helps the client evaluate his or her own behaviour and then helps them look for alternative ways of meeting the same needs.

The Choice Theory teacher knows that students who find the class work to be need-satisfying will not have recourse to disruptive behaviours.

The educational planner learns from Choice Theory that education is ultimately about helping people meet their needs better and on a life-long basis. The subjects and skills young people pick up at school enrich their quality worlds giving them access to a greater number of ways of meeting their needs.

The parent or teacher who has learned some Choice Theory no longer believes in attempting to control their children (or partners) and know that it is more satisfying relationships and more satisfying subject matter that work best.

Once you become aware of the existence of internal control, it is only gradually that you realise just how pervasive its importance is in your life and in all your relationships. This simple idea can take a long time to sink in!

Needs and Interventions

According to Glasser's Choice Theory psychology we all behave in order to meet our basic needs and we do this by choosing behaviours that enact our quality world pictures. These "pictures" represent the people, things, actions, events and values that we have stored in our memories as our personal ways of meeting our basic needs. Sometimes we may have pictures that are not very effective and/or not very respectful of the needs of others.

So, when a student "misbehaves" in school, that person is simply "behaving" in order to meet his or her basic needs. Although it is often important to curtail such behaviour for the good of others it is equally important to consider what is going on in the student's world. Why is his student behaving in this way? What need frustration is going on and what alternative ways might there be of satisfying this need?

Glasser's description of the basic needs and their function provides a very useful guide to this vital understanding of student behaviour and to intervening in a constructive way. What follows is an outline of the basic needs with examples of what some young people actually experience in relation to each need, typical behaviours they choose in an attempt to satisfy it and, finally, hints as to what adults might do to help the young person. The list is by no means exhaustive but hopefully it will give you a sense as to how this analysis can help guide more effective interventions,

BASIC NEED: Love and Belonging. Good relationships with others, genuine caring and human warmth.

Young person's experience: Chaos, neglect, attempted control, abuse, possessiveness, constant criticism, being bossed and pushed around, hostility, being ignored.

Behaviour chosen: Safety in gangs, cliques, seek peer attention, promiscuity, attention-seeking dress and appearance.

Adult intervention: Work with not against or over them. Avoid creating distance between you and them. Make a good relationship the number one priority. Do not construct walls of criticism! Help them relate better to their peers.

BASIC NEED: Power. Being able to do things of value, competency, self-confidence.

Young person's experience: Difficulty reading and writing, constant criticism and punishment, rarely listened to or respected, forced to learn what they see no need for, frequent experience of failure.

Behaviour chosen: Acting big, getting attention by any means, bullying, clowning, rebelling.

Adult intervention: Listen to them. Increase the sense of success in what they do offering small tangible steps ("learning zone"). Maximise and explain the relevance of learning material. Emphasise competence (grades A and B). See lesser grades as "not ready yet" rather than as "failure". Affirmation rather than praise or criticism. Contrive situations where they will experience success.

BASIC NEED: Freedom. Being able to run as much of their own life as possible and appropriate, have personal space.

Young person's experience: constantly being told what to do, often cramped living conditions at home, few people listening to them, confined to a school environment they do not understand.

Behaviour chosen: Escape, school avoidance, drugs, alcohol, self-harm, day-dreaming, lack of concentration, forgetfulness.

Adult intervention: Show an interest in what they want, give as much freedom as possible, encourage choices, help them understand the power of their own choices.

BASIC NEED: Fun. Very closely linked to learning, the joy of discovering new things and abilities, the excitement of living.

Young person's experience: Lack of leisure interests, unable to experience the fun of learning, often punished.

Behaviour chosen: Drugs, alcohol, vandalism, joy-riding, fooling around in class, hyperactive (often labelled as if it were an illness), giddiness.

Adult intervention: Seek moments of deliberate fun and welcome those that arrive uninvited. Foster learning with wonderment and excitement. Broaden their experience of leisure options.

BASIC NEED: Survival. Food, shelter, a home, warmth, comfort, health, nourishment, safety.

Young person's experience: Insecurity, hunger, unhealthy food and living conditions, aggression and abuse, drugs atmosphere, poverty, neglect.

Behaviour chosen: Fight and flight, distrust of adults, stealing, lying, constantly defensive, always in survival mode.

Adult intervention: Create a safe, secure, calm and welcoming atmosphere, help them learn and experience good nutrition, help them experience healthy exercise and pastimes, be someone they can trust.

Obviously, in real life the basic needs do not work separately from each other although they are presented separately above for simplicity sake. In real life any one experience could satisfy or frustrate more than one need at the same time. Activities that have the capacity to satisfy many needs tend to be the best for school planning purposes. For example, attending a school football match takes on extra significance when considered from the viewpoint of the basic needs. There is belonging in being part of the supporters, power in seeing the team play well (win or lose), freedom in being able to get a healthy break from the worries of life and fun in all the excitement of the game. There is an overall effect of enhancing the school as a need-satisfying place, somewhere that is worth investing one's time and effort in.

I recommend you to choose one student you know, one that is far from a model of good behaviour. Take each of the basic needs in turn and apply the above analysis. What is this student's current experience of this need? What is the student doing in a desperate attempt to satisfy the need? What could you or the school do to rectify this situation? This is not necessarily an easy task but if we continue to treat such students with remedies that actually add to their frustrations we are dooming ourselves and them to failure.

Kevin was a difficult student. He was actually quite a pleasant individual but his constant interruptions of class with funny remarks and chatter created problems for all his teachers. Many approaches had been tried but Kevin's banter continued. So much so that his behaviour was the topic of a meeting of his class teachers. I could see Kevin's school life had become frustrating. I had Kevin the very next morning and I decided I would try a different tactic.

About ten minutes into the class period Kevin had shown none of the usual signs of disruption. I approached him and asked for the address of his parents. He got very worried but gave me the details asking what I needed them for. I told him that I wanted to write to them but that I would show him the letter first and, if he did not like it, he did not need to deliver it. That both calmed and mystified him. Doing something different almost always has interesting outcomes.

From the far end of the room Kevin watched intently as I penned a few lines to his parents. What I said was the simple truth. I explained that I had Kevin for class today and that his behaviour was exemplary. (Had I waited a little longer I suspected I would have been unable to make the same statement.) I showed the finished letter to Kevin and he was stunned. I don't think he had ever received a report like this. He was delighted for me to sign the letter and he assured me he would bring it to his parents.

Later in the day I was to discover an interesting twist. At lunch-time, Kevin made a photo-copy of the letter for each of his teachers and delivered each copy with pride. As teachers we need to be good at working with less than half filled bottles!

If I were dealing with Kevin today I might use a different approach. I would invite him to write a brief note explaining how he was managing to work so well in the class today. This would help him focus on his own effort and at a time when this was being very effective. I could suggest that he show this note to his parents.

Need Satisfying Learning

If a school or its classrooms are not need-satisfying for our students then we have a problem on our hands. We ourselves quite rightly tend to avoid people, places and activities that do not meet our needs very well. Nobody wants to stay too long in a Fawlty Towers hotel! If there is any subject in a school that cannot be shown to be need-satisfying then we need to ask seriously why we have it in the school. Now that would be an interesting exercise!

Each one of our teachers has spent years studying History or Spanish or Physics or any number of other subjects. They have studied their chosen topics out of personal interest. That is not to say that all of their studies were equally satisfying. However, even the occasional boring lecturer or difficult part of the subject was not enough to dampen their enthusiasm since the bulk of the material was interesting for them.

We owe it to our students to share that enthusiasm with them, to show that the subject is useful and fascinating. As well as the subject matter we need to pay attention to the nature of the relationship we offer our students. Both the subject and the teacher need to be seen as need-satisfying by the students.

The following topics and related questions are intended to be a teacher's self-evaluation aid and are based on Glasser's approach to education.

1. Relationship

   Do you respect the student as another unique human being?
   Are you as teacher approachable, human?
   Are your interactions with the student work-centred or people-centred?

Do you get to know the student as an individual?
Do you come across as the sort of person students will want to listen to?
Do they see you as a need-satisfying figure in their world?

2. Engaging

Do you focus the tuition/learning process on the precise stage each student is at? ("Instructional Level " stretching between Confidence and Challenge.)
Do you attempt to reach individuals rather than groups?
Do the students have an overview of what the class/course is all about?
Do they understand? Is it safe for them to say they do not understand?
Does your enthusiasm for your subject show, your hunger for new learning?

3. Useful

How does the subject matter relate to real life, real jobs?
Where is it useful in the student's present life?
Do you encourage a discussion of "usefulness"?
Do students see the classwork as relevant?
Do you give them projects that focus on the subject's usefulness?

4. Meaningful

Is your classwork a complete experience, linking clearly with other topics?
Do students get the chance to experience the subject matter in a way that reveals its attractiveness, fascination?
Can it integrate with other subjects, courses?
Do you use "just-in-case" learning or "just-in-time" learning?

5. Experiential

Do the students get a chance to learn by doing, moving, presenting, getting involved, using a hands-on approach? (Constructivism)

6. Responsible

What choices do students have about their learning? What consequences apply?
Do students have some sense of control over how they learn?
Do they realise the learning belongs to them, not to their teachers?

7. Quality

Is quality or competence discussed, elaborated?
How do you apply grading schemes?
Are there clear goals?
How is progress measured? Who measures it?
Is student work displayed?
Do you help raise expectations, teach in a way that gives hope?
Do you help students take pride in reaching competence?

8. Variety

How much variety is there in your class? Telling, showing, involving, simulating, quizzing, challenging, surprising, sitting, standing, moving.
Do you cater for different learning styles and personalities? Auditory, Visual, Kinaesthetic ... and the myriad of new styles students present!
Do you surprise students now and again?

9. Positive

Do students receive affirmation, specific feedback on their progress?
Is there an atmosphere of optimism and hope?
Is self-esteem enhanced?
How do you process student "mistakes"?
Do you plan tests that encourage rather than discourage?
Is homework a carefully planned extension of learning or just a chore?
Does your approach reflect a belief in intelligence, emotional intelligence, multiple intelligence or infinite intelligence?
Is there laughter and humour in your class?

10. Collaborative

Is your role clearly collaborative, working **with** the student?
Is the student's role collaborative, part of a team where the strong help the weak?

An important dimension of teaching is being able to see something positive in the partially filled bottles of the students' lives. We need to be able to recognise progress even in the earlier stages of the learner's journey. The same applies to ourselves. If we really want to improve the quality of our teaching then we need to be patient with ourselves. Setting small concrete objectives for the coming week is more effective than making big plans we cannot keep.

Enhancing the Classroom Atmosphere

There are a number of relatively simple approaches that can greatly improve the classroom relationship, creating a more positive environment for our young learners and, indeed, for the teacher as well. Unlike almost any other job, a teacher faces a full "shop of customers" in each class period. The extras that add a quality sparkle to this busy environment need to be simple and brief.

Meet them at the door: Arriving before your students has many benefits (although many schools have not worked out how to arrive early without leaving the previous class early). Arriving early means you can help your students enter the room in an orderly manner, something that calms the environment right from the start. You can give your students a friendly welcome before starting the serious work of the class. Even more important is that you can target one or two students each time so that specific issues can be dealt with. Examples: "Sean, is your Mum out of hospital yet?" "Roisin, you kept your word and got here on time today!" "Jack, I'm counting on you to keep the deal we made last day."

The silent signal: As in many areas of human life it is an advantage to intervene at the warming up stage rather than waiting for the pot to boil over. A well-timed special look or hand signal can alert a student to potential problems before any damage is done. This preserves the good teaching relationship and averts crises. The signal can be discussed in advance with the student, a signal that can be made quietly without others noticing.

Make a deliberate mistake: Tell your class in advance that today you will make one or more deliberate mistakes during the class period. This helps them pay more attention and adds some useful fun to the exercise. (This idea came from the book,"The

Teacher's Toolkit".) Mistakes can be 2+2=5, "revollution", "As You Like It" by the Beatles. Have fun.

Use self-evaluation as much as possible: This means inviting students individually or in groups to evaluate their own work. Ask in a friendly way: "What mark would you give that out of a hundred?", "Are you happy with the work you have done?", "Is your essay ready yet or do you think you need to do more work on it?" At first students might not take the questions seriously but when they see you are treating them in a fair way they will be more honest in their self-evaluations and more keen to produce better quality work. It helps to add, "How can I help you do it better?"

When there is a problem, talk: Admittedly the often hectic pace of school life does not seem to provide a lot of space for talking and yet talking is vital. The "quick fix" is often the hardest one to repair later. If there is a problem with a student, indicate calmly that you will talk about it later. This gives time for the atmosphere to cool, time for both teacher and student to reflect on what happened, time to plan the chat. Equally important is that it gives the good example of sorting out things in a peaceful collaborative spirit, a lesson our world so badly needs. Talking is so important that some schools I know put a notice in each classroom: "When we have a problem, we talk!"

Vary your teaching style: There is a lot written nowadays about different learning styles. I do not believe it is necessary or advisable to invest time in analysing the specific mix of these that best suits your class group. Instead, if a teacher makes the effort to deliver content in a variety of approaches then the different learning styles will be well catered for and, in any case, variety is always appreciated. The "I talk/you listen" or the "I write/you copy" strategies get boring very quickly. The book, "The Teacher's Toolkit" is an excellent source of ideas about varying lessons.

Do the unexpected: Now and again do something completely different. Talk a little about your own life. Read a short extract from a book. Take the class for a short walk. Ask them what might happen if your particular subject were banned by law! Ask students what they are looking forward to.

Have Class Group Meetings: Now and again, encourage an open discussion by students about matters of general class concern - how well they are progressing towards examinations, topical issues and the like. Students benefit greatly from being listened to! The teacher gets to know the students at another level and the relationship flourishes.

Have a Party: Yes, a party! You might only have it once a year but that would be enough. Everyone could chip in a little cash and use the proceeds to buy fruit juices and snacks. Alternatively, the class could make a trip to a local eating establishment complete with teacher.

The Learning Zone

A Russian Psychologist, Lev Vygotsky, writing in the 1930s, claimed that all good teaching/learning takes place in what he called the "*zone of proximal development*" (ZPD). This lies between what the student **can do alone** and what the student **cannot do at all**. In other words it is what the student **can do with help**. He sees teaching as an active involvement in this "can do with help" zone. This is sometimes called the "instructional level" and I prefer to call it "**the learning zone**". The teacher is seen as providing scaffolding for this stretching of knowledge and skill that we call learning.

By way of illustration we can look at the "Reading Recovery Programme", an extremely successful approach to teaching reading that relies heavily on the learning zone. In each learning session the student is working with four texts (short readers) each at a carefully measured and adjacent level of difficulty.

A) a text the student is very familiar with, reads easily and enjoys the success.
B) a text the student has seen before and is now used to teach new skills.
C) a text the student has seen before and is used to identify learning needs.
D) a text the student has not seen before but some advance discussion of the contents whet his or her appetite.

The reader that is presented on a Monday at stage D moves to stage C on Tuesday and so on so that by Thursday it has reached stage A, something the student can do well and enjoy the success. Stages B and C would be the main learning zone.

We can adapt these ideas so that in one class we introduce a new topic briefly with an emphasis on stirring interest and some degree of familiarity. In the next class we bring up the topic again but with an emphasis on finding what the students already know and what they don't know, identifying the learning zone for this topic. In the following class we teach in this learning zone working with the students in a collaborative way. In the very next class we revisit the topic again but this time to enjoy the sense of achievement. In any one class session each of these four levels will be in operation.

The learning zone could be conceptualised as a special focus (represented by the black spot in the diagram below), something the teacher and student use to move through increasing levels of difficulty of the subject matter.

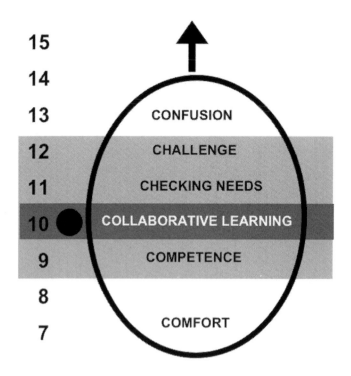

Today the learning focus may be on difficulty level 10 but today's work will also include consolidation of what was learned in level 9 as well as introducing level 12 for the first time. Level 11 will be used today in an exploratory way and tomorrow the focus will move up a level to eleven.

Areas of confusion or comfort are not useful parts of the focus of the learning interaction. The confusion zone is too difficult. The comfort zone is too easy and becomes boring.

If we give students work to do and they then complete it successfully without our help, they have not learned anything from us in Vygotsky's opinion. They are in their comfort zone and could become bored if they stay at this level for long. We need to start with what they can do (competence) and help them move towards what is challenging but not confusing.

It is interesting to consider how we define the upper and lower limits of the learning zone. Obviously a grade of 100% would indicate the content is too easy. Surprisingly the starting point, the lower level, is usually where the student would achieve about 95% success. The challenging or upper limit of the zone is where he or she would achieve only about 90%.

The narrowness of the learning zone and the high levels involved will surprise many teachers. We sometimes give student work that is too difficult, work that is in the challenging to confusing zone where most would score in the 40-70% range. This weakens their motivation and their belief in higher achievement. The learning zone approach focuses on material that gives challenge and a strong feeling of success. This improves motivation and helps students aspire to very high grades. Many will aim for 100%. The student feels positive about the material and so wants to learn more.

The Learning Zone	<90	CONFUSING	frustration
	90%	CHALLENGING	excitement
		CHECKING NEEDS	fascination
		COLLABORATIVE LEARNING	progress
	95%	COMPETENCE	confidence
	95+	COMFORT	boredom

Teachers often make the double mistake of starting too high and aiming too low. We need to start where the students are simply because they cannot start from anywhere else.   We also need to recognise their satisfaction in achieving success and the higher the better. The extremes of boredom and frustration are outside the learning zone.

One learning zone will not suit everyone in a class group but this imbalance can be addressed by having the more advanced students help those who are behind.

These ideas also have implications for assessment. We tend to think of tests as providing a grade as a measure of achievement but there are other aspects we might consider. We can use short assessments to determine what is the comfort zone for the student and what is the confusion zone. What do they already know and what do they need to learn? This helps us identify the learning zone (ZPD), the main target area of our teaching.

We can also build success into our assessment. If we give a student an in-class test where he or she will get a low mark we must consider the motivational effects of this. Why not construct a test early in the learning process designed so that most students will score 80% or more? Also tell them that if they want 100% you will help them achieve this. Then gradually over time the standard of the test increases and the students keep achieving over 80% until they are capable of achieving this level in State examinations.

The belief that giving students lowered grades scares them into working harder is unfounded and instead it tends to destroy confidence and even lives. Students will learn best if riding the crest of a wave of success, one that may start in shallow waters and then move to greater depth.

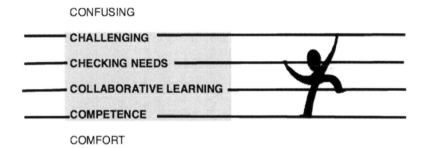

CONFUSING

CHALLENGING

CHECKING NEEDS

COLLABORATIVE LEARNING

COMPETENCE

COMFORT

An idea common to the Vygotsky approach is that of "scaffolding". The teacher provides a temporary structure which will help the student stretch and move upwards. The learning zone is a measure of the "reach" of this scaffolding. Scaffolding by its nature is temporary, is a form of external support, starts from the ground up, does not interfere with the building proper and is removed once the building is complete. The teacher creates this scaffolding by using different techniques at different levels, but all within the learning zone.

CHALLENGE

Encourage the students to think in terms of "stretching" upward, of constantly improving their level of competence. Ask them often what grades they would like to achieve.

CHECKING NEEDS

This can include the student's own self-evaluation: "What do you need to learn about at this point?" The process should not be presented as a search for faults but one of identifying areas to provide help or clarification.

COLLABORATIVE LEARNING

The teacher works **with** the student. "What do you need me to explain? How can I help you achieve your goals?"

COMPETENCE

The teacher will use this level to help the student's self-esteem, returning to it from time to time as necessary. Give students affirmation (e.g., "you have reached your goal") rather than praise ("you are fantastic!") about their competence. Emphasise effort rather than intelligence.

The traditional approach to teaching has tended to be "I do, you watch". Sometimes the process is "I do, you watch" followed immediately by "you do, I watch". These are important components of a more complete process where the learner moves from being helped to being independent. It is very much an example of the "leading out" ("educare" in Latin) that education is all about.

In order to respect the learning zone and the need to build up confidence gradually a more complete outline of the process would be:

I do, you watch >>> I do, you help >>> You do, I help >>> You do, I watch

Here is a simple example of what this might look like where a mathematics teacher is dealing with the topic of isosceles triangles.

I do, you watch.
The teacher shows the student how to draw an isosceles triangle.
The student observes.

I do, you help.
The teacher slowly draws another triangle.
The teacher prompts the student, "what do I do next?"

You do, I help.
The student draws a triangle.
The teacher prompts, "what do you do next?"

You do, I watch.
The student draws the triangle unaided.
The teacher observes.

A first encounter with these ideas may give the impression that they are too complex to use in practice. Think back about your own teachers at school. Those who taught you best would have been using a learning zone approach although it may not have been consciously worked out. The good teacher knows how to position students on the leading edge of the learning wave, that narrow line between comfort and confusion.

One way to focus on theses ideas is to take one topic, examine what aspects are too easy for the class, what aspects are too confusing and then plan the class around the material in between.

In the next section there are a few short exercises to help you consider the learning zone from a different angle and then to analyse at least one of your classes from this viewpoint.

Your Own Learning Zone

Understanding the significance of the learning zone may be helped by looking at your own learning. Let us suppose that in a burst of enthusiasm to improve the quality of your life you decide to go to four night classes that interest you. Here is how the first week turns out:

Spanish for Beginners: You find that all the other members of the class have called themselves "beginners" for the past five years and you are the only real beginner in the group, knowing a lot less than the rest.

Furniture Restoration: At the end of the week there is a short test of what you should know about furniture and you get a mark of 42%.

Art Appreciation: This week also ends with a short test about the week's work and you get a mark of 85%.

Advanced Word Processing: The teacher deals only with fonts, formats and spell checkers, all of which you could do in your sleep.

What would be your attitude to each of these courses after a week or so? How would you feel? Rate each of the courses from 1 to 5 using the three headings below where 1 is low and 5 is high. Circle the number that reflects your position.

Spanish
- your progress.   1-2-3-4-5
- Your enthusiasm.   1-2-3-4-5
- Your desire to continue 1-2-3-4-5

Furniture Restoration
- your progress.   1-2-3-4-5
- Your enthusiasm.   1-2-3-4-5

- Your desire to continue 1-2-3-4-5

Art
- your progress.   1-2-3-4-5
- Your enthusiasm.   1-2-3-4-5
- Your desire to continue   1-2-3-4-5

Word Processing
- your progress.   1-2-3-4-5
- Your enthusiasm.   1-2-3-4-5
- Your desire to continue   1-2-3-4-5

In your own recent teaching experience can you identify topics or even moments in class that match the following descriptions? You might like to note down brief examples of each.

1. The students already knew the material you intended to teach.
2. The students seemed interested as they teased out new knowledge (or skills) from what you were teaching.
3. The students seemed to have considerable difficulty in grappling with what you were teaching.
4. The students were completely out of their depth and were quite frustrated.

Consider one of your class groups and estimate how many students would fall into each of the 4 categories above. Overall how do you think your students would rate their experience of **your** classwork using the headings "Student's sense of progress", "Student's enthusiasm for the subject" and "Student's desire to continue"?

Students actually like to learn material that is presented in an interesting way. They learn less where the material is too easy or too difficult.

It would be an interesting exercise to give one of your classes a brief description of the three main layers of the learning zone (comfort - challenge - confusion) and invite them to rate recent topics according to these three levels.

The Reading Zone

The importance of being able to read is almost impossible to overestimate. Take the child who by the age of eight is reading comfortably at an age-appropriate level. Every single day after the reading threshold is reached new facts are being picked up from his or her environment: not only from books but also from signs, menus, text messages, the Internet, newspapers, advertisements, television. Through early reading foundations, are laid for more advanced learning. By the mid-teens, reading itself is taken for granted and the focus is on learning a wide selection of subjects and enjoying a wide range of leisure pursuits.

Now take the child who missed out, the one who did not achieve any useful standard of reading by age eight. A big part of the learning process is stalled and as each year passes, the accumulation of missing learning is of frightening proportions.

Marie Clay was a New Zealand teacher who decided to do something about such a problem. She created a system that came to be called "Reading Recovery". The results from this programme are impressive. Equally impressive (or maybe "depressive") is the number of people who attack the system denying that the Reading Recovery research is accurate or lasting.

So what does Reading Recovery do? First of all it is aimed at children's of 6 or 7 who are practically illiterate. The selection standard used in Ireland was to pick those children who knew two words or less. The goal of the system is to help these children learn to read to a standard as good as or better than their peers. For 98% of over 700 children included in the research, this goal was reached successfully and, for most of these, in a period of time of six to eight weeks. By any standard this is a remarkable success rate. It is easy to understand how some people can be sceptical but the research I quote is highly reliable and I have seen the system in operation at close quarters. So how does Reading Recovery achieve what it does?

The programme involves a one-to-one class of 30 minutes every day. During that class a very carefully planned series of learning experiences are facilitated for the child. The methodology links very closely to the ideas of Vygotsky mentioned in the previous chapter. The "learning zone" becomes very tangible in the selection of books that a child works with on any given day.

Book A is a new text that the child sees for the first time and the teacher helps the child gain some basic familiarity with the work.

Book B was yesterday's Book A but today it is the focus of the session's learning. The teacher helps the child become familiar with the new words, with the story and with reading it.

Book C was yesterday's Book B and is now treated as the familiar text. The student now has an opportunity to enjoy the material and rejoice in the very tangible increase in reading ability. In every single class the child is taken from a position of challenge to one of competence.

In a given lesson the teacher begins with the familiar book or books (Book C), moving to the book that is the focus of learning (Book B) and ending with a look at the new book (A).

The books used are real children's books that come in a range of shapes, sizes and attractive colours. The Reading Recovery team classifies these carefully into a grouping of about 30 levels. Classes are daily as it is vital to help the child catch up with peers as quickly as possible.

One major criticism people make of the approach is its cost. Thirty or forty private classes for one student requires a lot of money. Or does it? If a teacher charged €50 per class the total cost of the programme could be €2000 per child. For that amount of money the child is now equal to his or her peers as far as reading is concerned and can continue education on an equal footing. People sometimes pay more to straighten a crooked tooth and I believe that reading ability is certainly at least as important as the angle of a tooth. The cost of a two month one-to-one intervention must be compared to the cost of possibly six years of group learning and the cost to the individual of the delays in acquiring functional reading skills.

Another possible criticism of Reading Recovery is that it only deals with young children. A similar programme is very badly needed for those who reach adolescence with serious reading difficulties. However, Reading Recovery cannot be blamed for this lack as the onus of responsibility is on the educational authorities who deal with the adolescents.

Of course, it is more difficult to design a similar programme for this age group. It is not easy to find any reading materials that are of interest to this group and yet use very simple language. Another difficulty is that the longer reading is delayed the harder it becomes. However, without hard evidence I do not believe it is helpful to assume that reading difficulties are due to neurological factors. If a child still has reading difficulties by age ten there are many possible influences:

• Lack of early detection
• No early intervention
• Lack of accelerated intervention
• Attempts at reading associated with failure

• Lack of secondary skills acquired through reading

There is yet another factor and this has to do with the delay in acquiring any basic skill. It is well established that there is a decided advantage in learning certain skills such as playing a musical instrument or learning a foreign language at an early age. Brain scans reveal that more brain power is available for such skills if acquired early.   The same has to be true of reading skills but with reading there is even more at stake. The child whose reading is delayed also experiences delays in practically all other learning.

In conclusion I believe that no matter what age the child or young person are they will benefit from an intervention that is immediate, intensive, accelerated, age-appropriate, attractive, and professional. None of these attributes can be safely omitted.

If education is important and is a right then we can conclude that literacy, as the foundation of education, is the most fundamental skill to provide and protect.

More Effective Planning

One of the basic skills that everyone needs is planning. This can be as simple as how to arrange a few appointments tomorrow morning, how to combine study needs with leisure activities or something more complex such as putting together a major event. None of us is born with such skills implanted in our brains.

As young people move through our school system there is an increasing need for them to plan adequately and it makes sense to build some tuition on planning into their education. In this chapter all I hope to do is to introduce some general guidelines that could be shared and teased out with students.

The Characteristics of Good Plans

PREPARATION: Planning means working in advance and this in itself requires time. Make this clear to yourself by sitting down with pencil and paper.

PRIORITIES: What are the bigger issues that usually need to be addressed first? Spend some time determining the sequence of events.

POSSIBLE: Choose something you really can do and will do. Aim for at least 90% success. Absolutely anyone can tear a telephone directory in two ... if they tear out one page at a time!

PRECISE: Make the plan as specific as possible. Check out all the details: what? Where? When? Who with? How? For example: "What is the best time to talk to your friend about this?", "Where will you meet?", "How will you open the conversation?"

POSITIVE: Decide what you are going to do, not what you are not going to do. Aim to start something rather than stop something. Negative plans tend not to be effective.

PROMPT: Do it now … or even sooner! A prompt start maximises the time available if the plan needs to be adjusted or tried again and minimises the threat from unexpected interruptions.

PRACTICE: Rehearse what you are going to do. This builds confidence but also helps you spot problems in advance.

PROMISE: Make a strong commitment (not "I might", "I'll try" but "I will") to yourself. If you are saying, "I'll try" adjust your plan so that you can say, "I will".

PROTECT: Protect your plan. Anticipate potential sabotage. Get into the habit of doing what you plan to do.

PROCESS: Evaluate the effectiveness of your plan as you put it into operation and after you have completed it.

PERSEVERANCE: Keep trying. In the follow-up do not spend time on excuses, blaming, moaning or criticism. The only real failure is to give up trying.

Practising Planning

Once you grasp the idea of the characteristics of a good plan, it is a simple matter to draft some sample plans and invite students to comment on them in the light of the above characteristics. For example, "I am going to the centre of town with some friends this weekend". How could this plan be improved so that there is more likelihood that it will be successful? Which of the above characteristics are missing?

After one such short lesson on planning it is possible to refer back to the guidelines every time planning is needed subsequently.

Teaching Planning throughout the School

There are many topics such as this that can be introduced within a guidance or pastoral care programme but it is beneficial if the ideas are later reinforced throughout the school by other teachers. This applies to other topics such as learning skills, examination techniques and subject choice. Here is one way of doing this.

1.   Issue notes and/or a brief presentation to relevant staff members.

2.   Introduce the topic to the students and help them assimilate it through copious examples and practice.

3.   Remind the teachers that students now have the material and suggest ways they might emphasise this new learning in their classes especially in their next meetings with them.

Helping Students Learn How to Learn

Another vital life-skill is that of learning. We simply cannot assume that students know how to study, that is, to learn on their own. Learning is essential, not simply something relating to school. The ability to find, process and assimilate new knowledge and skills is an ability that is essential to personal as well as professional growth. It forms an important part of how we deal with new relationships and challenges in life whether it be mathematics, learning how to play chess or finding out how to paint a door. Learning is everywhere!

Of course, it is also necessary in the school environment. In a very real sense students' best (and worst) teachers are they themselves since it is their own ability to learn that is the final filter of information and skills into their lives. It makes good sense to help students build up their learning skills as early as possible. This needs to be done in a general way but also including an approach geared to each type of subject matter.

Key components of the learning cycle are: input (how the material is taken into the mind in the first place), storage (how it is linked to existing knowledge) and retrieval (how to access the information when we need it). If any one of these links is weak the whole process suffers. Later we shall see how a clever use of spider diagrams can help in all these stages.

Young people need help in learning about general strategies, about good work habits, study timetabling, study environment, summarising, revision schedules, pre-examination preparation, exam techniques. The LAST system (outlined below) is one general purpose strategy. It relies heavily on the idea of (1) absorbing the material well in the first place, (2) establishing a written summary and then (3) using that very same summary (be it diagram or text) over and over again.

Students will also need strategies that are specific to your own subject. For example, the use of diagrams in science or maths, the use of well-chosen key sentences in languages, the value of spider diagrams in essay-type subjects.

Teach Summarising

Learning is not about recording every detail of the subject matter. It is about storing key information that will later enable us to recall as much as we want or need of the subject matter. It is about summarising. I compare this to the use of instant coffee. We compress the coffee so that it is easy to carry and store. When we need it we expand it again by adding water. Summarising is just like that!

It helps to lead students through a typical learning exercise, helping them focus on the different stages of the process. You as the teacher think aloud as you process the material to be learned, expressing this in such a way that the students get an idea of what is involved.

- Give the students a short paragraph (maybe 20 lines) about a topic they are studying.
- Ask them what are the really important ideas in this paragraph.
- Then, what words or phrases could be chosen as key-words to represent these concepts?
- Ideally they should be able to underline these words (with a pencil).
- Each person might use different key phrases.
- Ask them to write these words on a separate page and invite them to reconstruct the paragraph contents from these words, without looking at the original paragraph.

• This helps them learn the value of key-words.

Teach Spider Diagrams

The next component to focus on is the structure of the topic. Invite the students to arrange the keywords on a page in such a way that they show how the paragraph is divided or structured.

Explain the idea of spider diagrams. An important aspect of these is that human memory works best with a maximum of three items so any one node of a spider diagram ideally should have no more than three branches.

Another feature of human memory is that images are easier to recall so encourage their use in the diagrams.

Doing a summary exercise like this from time to time teaches the students about summarising itself but also helps them learn the subject matter you use as an example.

From time to time encourage them to commit spider diagrams to memory and see if they can reproduce them on paper without reference to their originals.

These diagrams have been around for a long time and provide an individual with a graphic way of summarising ideas in such a way that they assimilate more easily into that person's thinking. For that reason it is vital that the person does his or her own spider diagram. Those made by others are not quite so useful and are often unintelligible to anyone other than their author.

First the person identifies keywords or concepts in the material to be learned, then jots these down in a diagram that shows how they divide and relate to each other. Such a diagram is also excellent for showing links to other ideas that may not be part of the current topic under focus.

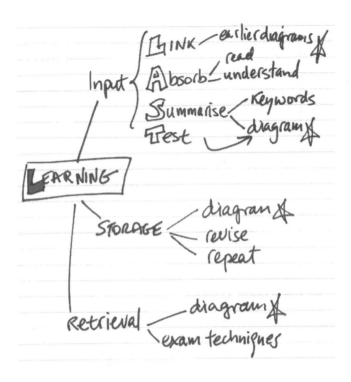

An important step in this process of using summaries is to encourage students to use that summary to give a brief verbal presentation of the topic. In other words, can they reconstruct and flesh out the ideas from the summary?

Emphasise the importance of keeping such diagrams in a safe place for future use. In fact any one diagram will have several uses.

1. As an initial summary of a topic.

2. By attempting the diagram from memory immediately after the topic study session the student

can check what has not been learned so well and can take instant action to fill in the gaps.

3. Several days later, when studying the next topic in the series, the student can redo the previous diagram as a way of linking the topics.

4. In pre-examination revision time the student once again attempts to do each diagram from memory and immediately fills in the gaps.

5. Then in the examination itself when a given topic appears in a question, the student can use the diagram to help formulate an answer.

6. Finally, in real life, if this topic is needed again the diagram will aid in recalling it.

Pop music can play an interesting role in study skills. Young people know the full lyrics of many pop songs (and even advertising jingles) but they rarely sit down to "study" such material. If only they could apply the same techniques to their academic subjects!

What happens is that (1) they hear the material many times and (2) it is always presented in the same format. Apply this to school learning. Go over the same material as often as possible BUT ensure that it is always in the same format! That is where the summary diagram is so important. It is vital to use the same diagram each time. Note that using summary diagrams made by other people is not so useful. One key aspect of such diagrams is that they are personal to the user, an individual's own personal way of assimilating new material into his or her existing knowledge.

The LAST Study Skills Method

If you go over something often enough you will know it! It makes sense to "go over" material in a way that improves the efficiency of your learning so that you do not have to re-learn absolutely everything later. Use these four steps.

LINK

- Before starting the new material revise the last few things you studied in this topic.
- Get an overview of what you are going to study so that you know where the different pieces fit it.
- Scan the new topic looking at headings and asking yourself questions about it.
- Find out how this topic links to earlier topics.

ABSORB

- Go slowly through the material aiming at understanding rather than speed.
- Ask questions about what you do not understand.
- Mark important points. Use a PENCIL!
- Add your own headings if necessary.
- Underline key words or ideas.
- Look up words you do not understand.
- You cannot remember what you have not absorbed!

SUMMARISE

- Identify the main key words or phrases and mark them.
- Make a very brief summary either as notes or preferably as a diagram.
- Keep this summary where you can find it easily again for revision purposes.
- A great help to learning is to view the material in the same format each time.

TEST

- Close the book and repeat the topic from memory.

- Better still write down your brief summary diagram of the topic.
- If you do not know the topic reasonably well just after studying it, you will have difficulty presenting it in an examination or using it in real life later on.

Study Skills Checklist

Successful Study doesn't just happen! There are definite steps you can take to make your learning more powerful, to improve your chances of a successful and happy study experience. However, there is not one set formula that works for everybody. This checklist is intended to do no more than assist you in identifying what is helping or hindering your study plans. Most of these have fairly obvious solutions and the next step is to plan and implement them.

OVERVIEW

1. Do you have a clear idea about the overall purpose of the course you are taking?
2. Do you have career plans?
3. Do you have a general understanding about what each of your subjects is all about?
4. Do you see learning as the teacher's job, your parents' job … or yours?
5. Does the new study environment or new timetable scare you a bit?
6. Are there other things going on in your life that makes study difficult?
7. Do you have problems with anxiety, panic, stress, memory-blanks, low self-confidence?
8. Do you find the prospect of all you need to do in your new course a bit overwhelming?
9. Is it proving difficult to fit in your course and study needs with the rest of your life?
10. Are your general health, eyesight and hearing functioning well?

11. Are you keeping all your needs in trim and in balance: belonging, power, freedom, fun and survival?
12. Do you see your teachers as people you can turn to for friendly advice and support?

INPUT

1. Do you have any special difficulties with reading or the use of English?
2. Do you attend classes regularly so as to get a good general grasp of what you need to study?
3. Have you got off to a reasonably good start in each subject and have a good foundation?
4. Are you lagging behind in one or more subject areas?
5. Have you a good system of note-taking and record keeping for learning from your classwork?
6. Do you know how to research a topic (e.g., library, Internet) and organise what you find?
7. Have you a good system for checking your own learning progress?

PROCESSING

1. Do you find it particularly hard to structure your independent study?
2. Have you an appropriate place where you can study in peace?
3. Do you set aside sufficient time each week for study or project work purposes?
4. Do you find it very hard to get started?
5. Have you a good system for learning new material?
6. Do you have a big problem with memory?
7. Do you have the computer skills that are useful for storing and processing your studies?
8. Are you good at summarising what you are learning?

9. Have you a good strategy for revising what you have learned?
10. Do you enjoy studying your subjects?

TIME

1. Do you tend to leave a lot of things to the last minute ... or "tomorrow"?
2. Do you keep running out of time?
3. Do you have a good practical approach to planning your study time?

OUTPUT

1. Do you have a problem expressing your ideas in spoken or written form?
2. Do you have the computer skills needed for good presentations and documents?
3. Do you have a lot of difficulty in preparing an essay or project?
4. Do you have a good examination preparation strategy?
5. Have you a clearly thought out approach that you use during examinations to maximise your grades?
6. Do you perform poorly in examinations in spite of knowing the material fairly well?

It is a good idea to complete this questionnaire and then discuss the results with your guidance counsellor.

Examination Techniques

As you prepare for an examination, to some extent you temporarily abandon the real reason for study at all which is some form of self-improvement through learning skills and knowledge. Formal assessments are necessary of course but the examination process is very different from the learning process. In the months prior to an exam it is worthwhile focusing on the specific requirements of this evaluation of learning.

Before the Examination

Apply for the examination: Make sure your name is down and all fees are paid and make certain that the correct subjects have been listed for you. The School Examination Secretary will have your details.

Keep up with your class group: Doing today's work today is difficult. But if you are not doing it you are not on target for examination success.

Don't give up: No matter how little time and how much work appears to be left you have a choice about studying or not between now and the examination. If you need help on how to study go get it. Be careful with thoughts of repeating. Many use this as an excuse for taking things easier now. Even if you really were going to repeat, hard work now will make the repeat more successful. The real measure of how hard you are working is how much you are prepared to do TODAY, not the promise of work tomorrow.

Aim to over-learn: If you are learning the minimum all the time you never really get to the "meat" on a subject, the material that makes it really interesting and worth learning. Once you have the basic work under control, reading special magazines about the subject or seeing TV programmes about it can help extend your knowledge and interest. Occasionally you may need to study hard at a subject you do not particularly like simply because you need it to enter a course. Acknowledging this fact can make the decision to work a little more attractive.

Get familiar with examination papers: Study old examination papers paying attention to the typical instructions that are given. Get to know the type of choices you will have. Find out if you are allowed extra helps such as calculators and what special instruments you might need for the examination. Good preparatory work in this department will make it easier (and faster) for you to process the instructions at the start of the examination itself.

Handwriting: If your handwriting is not too clear or is messy in appearance get some help now. Handwriting does not improve over-night but putting a little effort into it now can be a great help. Usually bad handwriting can be improved a lot by making one or two small changes. The examiner cannot give marks for anything he or she cannot read. If it is legible but hard to read or has a messy appearance the examiner might be less positive about your work.

Study-methods: Few people like to study but know it is necessary. It makes sense to get as much benefit as possible from the time you spend in study. There are methods such as the LAST system that can help you get more out of your time. Get help on study skills if this is a problem for you.

Planned revision: A good study approach will include planned revision. The simplest way is to spend 5 minutes revision every time you study a subject or do its homework. Contrary to popular belief it is more beneficial to revise before other work rather than after it as this helps establish links with earlier learning. You will learn ways to do effective revision when learning study skills.

Recreation: When you work hard, play hard. One good night off each week is a good idea. Do something that is fun and where study is not mentioned. Alcohol and examinations do not mix. The effects of alcohol in the body can continue for days afterwards weakening our perceptions, our thought processes and our memories as well as disturbing our sleep process.

Your physical health: Eat good wholesome food and in healthy amounts. Get adequate exercise and relaxation. Swimming is a particularly good activity for examination time. All forms of drugs, including those permitted by the law, are likely to impair your examination performance.

Count-down to Exams

In the last few weeks it is important to strike a balance. A good strategy is vital. Here is an example:

- Take one subject at a time.
- Take one topic at a time.
- Use a quick check of the book or notes (especially any summaries you have made) to identify your weak points.
- Brush up on these weaknesses.
- Briefly test your overall knowledge of the topic using summary diagrams.
- Again fill in obvious gaps.
- Keep all your diagrams and summaries for very last minute memory touch-ups.

Cramming: Everybody does last-minute studying but this can do more harm that good if some basic rules are not followed. Last-minute study should be about revision and filling the gaps. It is not about starting from scratch. Marathon study sessions can weaken your immune system leaving you wide open to extremely untimely health problems in the midst of your examinations.

Don't reduce sleep time: Last-minute study that uses up your sleep time is also taking away the energy and alert memory you need for your examinations. Lack of sleep can lead to tiredness, panic attacks, memory blanks and sloppy work.

The Day of the Examination

Have a shower: Many of your examinations will take place in the summer and so the weather can be quite warm. Have a shower or bath each morning of an examination. This helps you feel fresh and confident going into the examination centre. Use your favourite perfume, after-shave, etc., to help boost the "feel-good factor". Returning to the summer-time theme, avoid getting sun-burnt! It is never a good idea but it is even less welcome at examination time.

Dress wisely: Wear clothes that are clean and comfortable. Be able to add or remove layers if the temperature becomes uncomfortable during the examination. It is not a good idea to wear new clothes or shoes for the first time at an examination.

Bring your "kit" every day: This includes pens, pencils, eraser, calculator, set-squares, compass, spare refills and batteries. Make sure that everything you bring has been tried and tested beforehand. Why not get it ready now? You may also need your examination card and some form of identification. Keep your "kit" ready in a bag that you will bring to every examination.

Get the day and time right: Take down your time-table carefully or, if given a printed copy, mark your own examinations clearly. Check that you have understood the time-table by talking with friends and teachers. Each day ask your friends, "What do we have next?"

Be on time: Aim to be at least 20 minutes early! Being on time means not being flustered or worried about being late, not hurrying and building up a sweat. Being on time means having the space to make new plans if something goes wrong. It also gives you some minutes before the examination to get your thoughts in order.

Go to the loo: Make a visit about 10 minutes before you are due to enter the examination hall. Go easy on last minute drinks as this can cause discomfort during the examination.

Snacks: Provided they do not make noise or cause other disturbances, a packet of your favourite sweets on your examination desk can be useful. Even more important is to have drinking water.

During the Examination

Set aside planning time at the beginning: Ten or fifteen minutes planning time at the start is important. Make sure you have been given the correct paper and at your chosen level. Read the instructions carefully, even if they look the same as previous papers. Understand how many questions you are required to do from each section if given a choice. Read through the questions carefully and tick the likely questions for you to do. As you read questions jot down any ideas that come into your head.

If during your study you have built up good habits of summarising this will come in useful here as you will know how to make quick summary answers. Choose the questions you can get the most marks from, not necessarily the ones you like best. Decide how much of the available time you will give to each question making sure that this is in proportion to the marks for that question. Write the amount of time on the paper beside each question. Then, to help you judge your progress, write the estimated time of completion of each question.

Do each question carefully: Read each question several times. (A big number of students get low marks simply because they mis-read or misunderstand the question.) Start each new question on a new page if possible and number questions clearly. Plan your answer before you begin to write it. Work through the question carefully keeping an eye on the time. Don't worry if you are running a little overtime on an answer but be aware of the need to catch up later. The main thing is to have a sense of time.

Lay out your answers with lots of clear headings and spacious margins. Use diagrams and maps where possible but don't spend too long on colouring in these. In the case of calculations your rough work is important so keep it clear. Remember that you will often get marks even for a few words or lines. Blank spaces get nothing. If you have a number of items left to answer but you really do not know the answers, guess. Intelligent guessing is smart and deserves marks.

Check afterwards: Allow 5-10 minutes at the end of the examination for checking. Did you do the right number of questions? Have you followed the instructions exactly? If you have time to spare use it to check your spelling and grammar. Make neat corrections.

Learn to cope with the unfamiliar: Remember that even your own name sounds odd on the lips of a stranger! The examination questions may sound very unfamiliar as they are written by someone different from your teacher. Do not be put off and calmly translate the questions into terms you are familiar with.

Know how to cope with memory blanks: This can be part of panic or tiredness or, very often, both. Fighting against it or worrying increases the tension and prolongs the blank. The simple advice is DO SOMETHING ELSE USEFUL. Do another question, draw margins, check earlier work, re-do answers in a neater way. Your memory will probably come back and you will have made progress meanwhile. By the way, cramming, lack of sleep and the use of any kind of drugs all increase the chances of this happening.

Know when to leave: After working for so many years for your subject it does not make sense to waste any of the precious minutes provided to test your knowledge. If you do finish before the designated time, use this opportunity to check that you have followed the instructions correctly. Check your answers including spelling and grammar. Re-write answers and re-do diagrams where time permits you to improve the content or lay-out.

Between Examinations

Post-mortems: Certainly discuss the examination afterwards, if only to lay it to rest! Be warned however. Neither your feelings nor those of your classmates are to be trusted when it comes to how well you did. Very often a person feels great because in fact she has been able to write down everything she knows (however little that may be). Another student feels terrible because he did not write down everything he knows.

If all your fellow students are saying that a particular examination seemed very easy or very hard, remember that examiners usually make adjustments for both these situations so that at the end of the day it does not matter too much. All the candidates are in the same boat.

And onwards …. Before settling down to study for the next examination do something that gives you a good break. A great therapy for exams is a good swim but everyone has their own favourites. A reasonable amount of physical activity helps shake out tensions in the body.

Teenage Sleeping Habits

Typical scenario: Mum calls teenage son. Son grunts and turns over in bed. Mum calls son again, loud, angry. Son grunts loud, angry. A row begins. Mum getting desperate. Pulls bed-clothes off son. Day begins with a fight for both of them! Not a good start!

A school's support staff and teachers in general are well-placed to pass on some tips about good sleeping habits to the teenagers themselves or to their parents.

A teenager may find it difficult to get out of bed for a number of possible reasons:

1. Not had enough sleep during the night.
2. Not used to having personal responsibility for getting up.
3. Influenced by consumption of alcohol or other drugs.
4. Has a problem at school that she wants to avoid.

1. Ensuring that the teenager is getting enough sleep.

Length of time: most teenagers need between eight and a half and nine hours sleep per night. A fixed bed-time and making it a routine can help this. If a person is consistently getting less sleep, say, seven and a half hours, it is better to change gradually rather than move suddenly to eight hours.

Unwinding: it is important at night to unwind gradually before sleeping. This means reduced activity, low lights, low stimulation. Factors that can lead to disturbed sleep are: strenuous activity, food (especially the spicy variety), worries, fear, drinking liquids less than 90 minutes before bed-time, studying, video/DVD/TV/games in bed-room, illness. Some mobile phone makers, aware of the effects of very white or blue light have introduced ways to ensure that the phone gives a warmer more subdued light at night (and there are apps that achieve the same effect). Better still, do not use the mobile phone at night.

Reading something light in bed can act as a buffer between the day's activities and a good night's rest. Never study (or work) in bed. Watching TV in bed will not help sleep (though you may fall asleep watching it and then have disturbed sleep due to the blinking light and the sound). Listening to music or radio with headphones carries the same risks. Bedrooms are not good places for exciting equipment such as televisions and computers. If a young person does need to study in his or her bedroom then arrange the furniture as far as possible so that the bed is not visible from the desk and the desk is not visible from the bed.

Insomnia: if you wake up during the night it does not mean you are not getting rest. In fact we all go through different phases of sleep in any one night. Each phase lasts about 90 minutes and the individual gradually goes into a deeper sleep and then returns gradually to the surface. Sometimes a person wakes up briefly during these returns to lighter sleep. This is quite natural and does not indicate a lack of sleep.

Making an effort to go asleep will not work (since sleep is the opposite of effort). Just relax, enjoy being in bed, think about relaxing things. If you are horizontal and not twisting and turning you are getting rest. When the body really needs sleep it is hard to stay awake. If you do not like the dark, keep a torch by your bed instead of leaving lights on. If worry about something keeps you awake then it may be good to talk to someone about your worries and plan to do something about fixing the causes. Some people find it useful to have a jotter and pencil near the bed so that notes about worries or things to do later can be written down during the night.

Disturbed sleep: There may be something happening during the night that regularly disturbs a person's sleep. It may be traffic, cold spells during the night, family members or neighbours returning home late. It could also be unwelcome text or voice messages on the mobile phone. It may require some detective work to detect these as we are not always consciously aware of them.

2. Getting the teenager out of bed in the morning

Responsibility: The real problem here is usually that a parent or guardian is taking responsibility for getting junior out of bed and so the young person never learns how to get up in the morning. The teenager also rejects the external control and this can damage the parent/child relationship. The solution is to place the responsibility where it belongs, that is, with the teenager.

Alarm Clock: All teenagers should have their own alarm clocks. Find one that meets your needs. A high frequency alarm sound is usually better than a low frequency one. On the other hand a radio-alarm that will awaken you to the sound of your favourite music may be your preference. The alarm should be accurate, reliable and audible. If using the "snooze" feature works for you then use it. (Some mobile phones have very good alarm features.) An alarm sound that would be worthy of a fire-engine is probably not the best way to start the day! Like modern telephone sounds, the alarm should be inviting rather than threatening.

Getting up: The second step is to put the teenager in charge of his or her alarm clock and the getting up process. That means that if the young person oversleeps then they get to school late and must face the consequences of this for themselves. It is unlikely that your son or daughter will be late more than once in these circumstances.   In any case, learning about consequences is almost more important than learning about sleep.

Transport: If parents normally give the teenager a lift to school or to the bus stop then they must be very clear about the conditions.   For example, to get to school on time let's suppose you need to leave the house by car at 8 a.m. You as parent will have the car available at that time but no later. After the limit time your student must find his or her own way to school. You might offer an emergency lift to the nearest bus-stop but have clearly defined limits for this, for example, the emergency lift might be available up to 8:15 a.m. It is important to make your own very clear conditions and then to stick to them. Otherwise junior will not learn to take responsibility for getting up. You have other responsibilities of your own at the beginning of the day and teenagers are quite capable of getting up and going to school on their own.

Consequences: If your son or daughter gets into trouble for arriving late to school, it is the teenager's problem, not yours. Do not write any notes excusing the delay. Hopefully junior will only experience this lateness once!

Relationship: It is absolutely essential that criticism and nagging are absent from this process. Explain it clearly to your son or daughter and do so in a friendly way.

3. Possibility of alcohol or substance abuse

Sometimes the first warning signal that a parent gets about their child experimenting with drugs is the change in sleeping patterns. If you suspect that this is the case it is a good idea to get professional help.

4. Avoidance of a school problem

One of the first signs you may get of a serious school-refusal problem is that your son or daughter does not want to get up. This refusal can be particularly strong on Monday mornings and on the first day back after a holiday break. The refusal may be disguised by complaints about illness. Some of these, such as stomach pains or a headache may be the very real by-products of anxiety.

Do not get into an argument about school-refusal. Once the school start time is past contact the school and let them know that your son or daughter has refused to go. Do not make any excuses for them. If under the school-leaving age the child will then come to the attention of the Educational Welfare Board. If over that age you may need to have a serious discussion with your teenager about plans for the immediate future.

Guidance counsellors can set up a scheme where the young person commits to going to school each day but spending the day in the counsellor's office. This temporarily removes whatever is threatening to the student and provides an opportunity for counselling support. In my experience, a visit by the student's friends at break time could be very important in encouraging a return to the classroom. (Typical reasons for school refusal include bullying, or teasing, lack of friends or social skills, academic difficulties, fear of individual teachers, self-consciousness in changing rooms, fear of examinations.)

Career Clusters

The career preparation of young people starts early in their education when they hear about many different occupations and interests. Somewhere between that initial browsing of different careers and a final career choice there needs to be a gradual process of homing in on a specific career area. I deliberately say, "career area" since it is generally not be a good idea for a teenager to claim to have found his or her life's career in too definitive a way. Career choice is quite different from job choice.

In the years immediately following secondary education young people are very much finding their own identities through greater independence from their families of origin. What appeared to be a wonderful career choice at seventeen can be viewed very differently two years down the line. Equally significant is that nowadays people will often have several careers, even combining several career strands at the same time in their lifetime. These considerations would suggest that young people identify one or more general areas of interest rather than a specific occupation.

General Preparation for Careers

If school is to some extent a preparation for life then it must also be a preparation for careers. This is not an easy focus for teachers who understandably want their students to do well in each subject examination but this broader view is essential. If we take any categorisation of careers and apply it to school life we can see where there are gaps in this preparation that young people are receiving and we can take steps to improve it by changing the range of subjects on offer and/or by increasing the number of extracurricular interest groups in the school.

For example, to use my adaptation of the six categories of John Holland's RIASEC system, here are examples of school activities which might enhance a student's experience of different career directions. Once we consider educational goals in this broader context we find that many activities that are regarded as peripheral to school life are in fact quite important.

MANUAL: careers involving moving and lifting things, often outdoors, requiring good physical fitness e.g. carpenter, mechanical engineer.
School activities: Woodwork, Metalwork, Technology, Art, Crafts, Agriculture, Home Economics, Physical Education, Sport.

UNDERSTANDING: careers where it is important to know how and why things happen, scientific, research. Eg. quality control, electrician.
School activities: Mathematics, Physics, Chemistry, Biology, Home Economics, Photography, Video, Magic.

ARTISTIC: where beauty and its expression is important, words, graphics, movement, drama. Examples: dancer, novelist.
School activities: Art, Music, Choir, Crafts, Drama, English Literature, Dance,

SOCIAL: lots of direct supportive contact with people. Examples: childminder, social worker.
School activities: History, Physical Education, Fund Raising, Sports, Peer Counselling.

INFLUENCING: organising events and people, selling, persuading. Examples: advertising, Army Officer.
School activities: Commerce, Mini-companies, School shop, Fund Raising, Guidance Committee.

CLERICAL: Dealing with papers, office machines, computers. Examples: Computer operator, Accountant.

School activities: Information Technology, Programming, Commerce, Keyboard skills, Guidance Committee.

It is equally important to invite students to analyse their own life experiences using categories such as the above to see how many different career areas they have sampled in some way. The one they have omitted might be the most important one for them. Each category can have several different sub-headings: work experience, school subjects, hobbies and interests, special strengths. Learning how to do this analysis is something that will be useful to them in later life at any time they need to evaluate their own career development.

Career interest tests and questionnaires are helpful but they should be seen as the start of a process of self-exploration rather than the end of that process. It is advisable to use several of these so that no single set of results is conferred with an aura of infallibility. Aptitude tests should be used in a similarly tentative manner with the resulting discussion and self-appraisal being more important than the actual scores.

In adult guidance there is usually some degree of urgency in linking career interests to a specific job application. With young people, on the other hand, we strive to keep their interests broader as they gradually focus on what is most suitable for them. Closing the exploration door too soon is not helpful.

Career Choice

In the final count-down months young people need to make more specific career choices in order to have definite plans for the years following their secondary education. There are three general strategies that can be useful here: browsing, scanning and probing. These do not necessarily happen in a linear sequence but each stage has its own type of resources.

Browsing: In the first place career planning requires a lot of browsing, becoming familiar with a big range of very different careers. The Internet makes this a lot easier than in former times but both guidance counsellors and teachers can encourage the browsing component by setting challenges for students. Approach this from different angles: What careers have height requirements? Which jobs require good physical fitness? Name careers beginning with the letter "P". How many different careers can you spot in tonight's soap opera episode? General talks from people talking about their own careers with a space for student questions can form part of the browsing dimension.

Scanning: At this stage, young people need to be able to compare one career with another. To this end they can learn about a set of standard parameters they might use in scanning: Entry requirements, qualifications required, main activities involved and so on. It was for this specific stage that QualifaX was created about thirty years ago and we are fortunate in having several different career and course scanning utilities on the Internet of today. Students can be encouraged to select two or three courses or careers and compare them using the same set of parameters for each. Scanning becomes increasingly important as the person begins to focus on specific career areas.

Probing: This stage is where the career planner looks into a final short list of careers or courses in some depth. Detailed information about a course and its related careers is vital at this level but it is not enough to rely simply on written documents. Young people need to sample the courses and careers they are considering. Not to do so would be a serious omission in choices that require a big investment of time and money. They need to be able to give a good realistic answer to the question, "what would it be like for me to be doing this all day every day?" Sampling can include work experience, visits to colleges of further training and education, shadowing students in those colleges, interviewing workers, engaging in social media groups involving careers of interest.

Counselling: A vital component of the latter scanning and probing phases of career exploration is individual career counselling. However, it makes for greater efficiency to do as much career guidance as possible in a group context leaving counselling for the fine-tuning of the more personal aspects of career choice and planning.

Career Events

As teenagers' career interests begin to crystallise there is an extra challenge for the guidance counsellor in delivering a guidance programme. Those who are interested in apprenticeships will be quite bored by long presentations about university entrance and the university aspirants are equally disinterested in apprenticeship information. So how can this be managed?

One way is to work on the basis of career clusters. After an initial phase helping students identify their major career areas of interest (using the MUASIC system, for example), students can be clustered into each of the categories for further career exploration. It is important that they should feel free to move from one category to another and explore more than one category.

In a guidance class context these clusters can form project groups, each supplied with a range of career brochures. For example, an artistic cluster could have brochures about drama courses, interior decoration courses and English literature courses. They could be set the challenge of identifying the specific occupations that such courses would lead to, analysing the pros and cons of each. As the students progress and become interested in specific groups of courses, these clusters can reform around similar courses to explore and exchange information together.

When career or course representatives are invited to the school, it can be useful to have several of these at the same time but in different rooms so that students can opt to attend the talks they are most interested in.

A model we found very helpful for evening career events for senior students was to have three sessions. (We normally shared career events with the six second level schools in Drogheda, a policy that made it easier to have a bigger selection of career representatives.)

In the first of the three sessions about six different presentations were available and in separate rooms. Ideally these represented a wide variety of career types. The time for each session was 40 minutes and the presenters were advised to speak for no more than 15 minutes leaving the rest of the time for the students to ask questions. This helped guarantee that the talks would meet the needs of the students. In some cases the individual session might include two brief presentations on related areas.

The second session was a repeat of the first so that any one student could attend two different presentations. The presenters could stay in their original rooms throughout the career event but the students could move around.

For the third session it was open house. All the room doors were left open and students could roam around freely visiting each career they might be interested in. In this way a student could attend two detailed career presentations and later explore several other options.

For juniors a different format was used and here we arranged our presenters in what we called the "market-place layout". As big a range of careers as possible was represented and each one was assigned to a table. They were encouraged to make their "stall" as attractive as possible, bringing posters and artefacts illustrative of their career areas if they could. They could simply take questions from the students or could give very brief presentations, about 5 minutes, to groups of students. The main objective was to enable students to visit or see as many different careers as possible. Very often a student would visit the guidance counsellor weeks after such an event to enquire further about a career they had first seen at this career evening.

One thing that is fundamental in career guidance: every child's career is important. With that in mind we need to maintain an openness to the vast array of possible careers in the world of today. Equally we need to be aware that many of our young charges might well create totally new careers in the future that do not exist today. When you meet ex-students and enquire about their careers and find that you do not fully understand their answers, you know that you are dealing with new careers that were never to be found in the career leaflets of old or in the lists of suggestions arising out of career interest tests. That is how our world is evolving.

Certainly the ultimate measure of a school's success should not be based on the number of university places achieved nor indeed in the number of apprenticeships but in the quantity of happy and successful young adults who have found careers and ways of life that are fully satisfying to them.

The Hidden Problems of Students

The Hidden Issues

Due to the restraints of confidentiality it is quite difficult to transmit to our teaching colleagues some of the problems we deal with in our counselling offices. At the same time it is important for them to realise that they deal with these same problems without always being aware of it. Communicating this information to them in some form will help them approach teaching in an even more human way and will also help them understand our work. Even more important is that it will help them develop greater sensitivity to the young people who fill the desks in their classrooms.

In Glasser's Choice Theory psychology he claimed that all of us are always choosing the best we know at the time. Why would anyone do otherwise? This does not mean we are necessarily choosing what is really best for us or for anyone else. It simply points out that in our own view of the world we are making the best choice we possibly can.

That means that the child who is throwing paper aeroplanes from one side of the classroom to the other during a lesson on the structure of the atom is in fact choosing the behaviour that appears best to satisfy his or her needs at that moment in time. If this is true then the only really satisfactory way of dealing with such behaviour is firstly to understand where it is coming from and secondly to address that underlying frustration. A simple prohibition of the offending behaviour (or punishment of same) does nothing to address the underlying cause.

The exercise outlined below was designed for a presentation to teachers to help them understand what might be going on in the lives of their students. The activity can be completed in about 15 minutes. It doesn't lecture anybody ... it simply throws up different points of view. What follows are typical instructions but you may adapt them to suit your own situation.

In advance of the activity print out the material in the "Cards" section below and then cut up the paper so that each numbered paragraph ends up as a separate card.

Typical instructions follow in quotes: "I need twelve volunteers. All I will be asking each person to do it to read out a short paragraph."

When you have the volunteers give each one card. Give them out in random order.

"What you are going to hear will give you some insight into the types of students we come across in guidance counselling. It will also give you another view of students that you may be teaching. It is important to mention that what you will hear now is not based on real students in this school but on a collection of experiences by other guidance counsellors. The data is disguised but the types of cases are real."

"First I am going to introduce you to person A. Would the teacher holding card A1 please read out what you have.
The teacher with A2 .... " [and so on]

It is probably not necessary to discuss this very much but a space for comments or questions at the end may be helpful. Teachers will want to know what they can do to help such students.

When the exercise is finished ask the volunteers to destroy the papers since some students finding them could think that their individual confidentiality had been breached.

The Cards

A1: I teach Mary and I can't do anything with her for the last few weeks. She's moody and aggressive. I had to bring her to the Principal the day before yesterday because she told a young fellow to f**** off. She hasn't done a single piece of homework for ages. She sets a bad example and I don't like her in my class.

A2: Mary is my daughter. She just spends all her time in her room and only answers us with grunts. If I ask her about her homework she just storms out of the room and slams the door. Her moods affect the whole family.

A3: I'm Mary. About a month ago, on a Sunday night, I was raped. I don't know what to do or who to tell. My Mum will blame it on the drink. My Dad will say I should have been home earlier. I think I'm going crazy!

B1: This is Jake, a student of mine. He has a violent temper, flies off the handle for the least little thing. At other times he is a good student.

B2: Jake is my eldest son. His step-father, who's been around since Jake was one year old, gets on very well with him. Since he turned thirteen Jake has got very moody. It's the teenage thing I suppose.

B3: I'm Jake. I just need my Dad, my real Dad, to call me, just once. I need to know why he left me, why he's not around, why he doesn't call. I don't want to ask my Mum as it might upset her. I don't know who can help me.

C1: Roisin is my student. She never has any homework on a Friday. In fact she's never on time on a Friday either and gives all sorts of silly excuses. I'm convinced she's lying through her teeth. I think she probably stays up half the night watching videos to judge from the bags under her eyes.

C2: Roisin is my second eldest. She's always answering me back. I think it's the company she's keeping. She hasn't been the same since she went to secondary school. Her Dad and I are very worried about her.

C3: I'm Roisin. My Dad gets paid every Thursday and then drinks himself stupid that evening. We all lie awake afraid of what he's going to do when he gets home. We sleep in our clothes in case we need to get out of the house. Sometimes he throws chairs at us. My Mum's just as much afraid as we are. We called the police once and he only got worse after that. We don't know what to do. I can't tell anybody. I'm ashamed. I'm scared!

D1: Here's Harry, probably the best student I have at the moment. His work is always done to perfection and, when I ask him a question in class he always knows the answer, though in recent times he seems a bit reluctant to answer.

D2: Harry is definitely the best behaved of my three children. He's very close to his Mum and can be full of chat when he's around her. He's really good at his studies. Unlike the others, we never need to get him to tidy his room as he's tidier than we are.

D3: I'm Harry. Nobody in my school ever speaks to me. They tease me, call me a "teacher's pet". Often they push me around. I can't take it anymore. I am going to kill myself.

How Teachers Can Help

- The single most important thing is to be a good listener.

- Students need to know that, if they try to talk to you, you will be receptive.
- Let your students see you as human and compassionate.
- Be a good observer. Note changes in student moods or behaviour.
- Become familiar with behaviours that suggest underlying problems.
- Learn about the law and ethics of reporting suspected problems.
- If you are unsure seek advice sooner rather than later.
- If you suspect that a student may have a personal problem be discreet in how you mention this to the student.
- Pass on your concerns to the guidance counsellor.

Behaviours to Monitor

I do not believe it is very helpful to treat psychological problems in the same way doctors treat physical health problems. There is no accurate matching of symptoms to underlying psychological issues. However, there is a range of behaviours and circumstances that might suggest that all is not well and the purpose of what follows is to help draw attention to these "symptoms".

Teenagers probably vary their moods and conduct more than any other age group but this list attempts to identify the more extreme behaviours or changes in behaviour that may indicate some underlying problem. If you detect these changes you are recommended to discuss the student with the guidance counsellor to see if a referral is advisable. If you become aware or suspicious of any serious problem (e.g., epilepsy) inform the year head or counsellor; do not assume that other staff members know.

General Behaviours

- unhappiness
- pattern of absences or erratic attendance
- isolating behaviour (avoiding other students)
- outbursts of anger or aggression
- hyperactive behaviour
- hygiene issues
- excessive need for toilet visits
- unusual thirst
- unusual mood-swings
- very low self-confidence, pessimism
- repeated attention-seeking (good or bad)
- trance-like behaviour
- slurred speech
- confused thinking, communication
- bizarre behaviour (e.g. inappropriate sounds, constant hand wringing)
- eccentric behaviour
- essays that have unusual content
- associating with groups on the fringes
- frequent rule-breaking
- difficulties with authority, correction
- sense of "being picked on"
- talking a lot about death
- inappropriate sexual references
- expressions of hopelessness, "what's the use?", "nobody cares"
- giving away prized possessions

Appearance

- poor eye-contact
- unkempt
- blushing
- unhealthy appearance
- regular tiredness
- under-nourished

Suspicions

- bullying, being bullied
- substance abuse
- physical abuse
- sexual abuse
- emotional abuse
- promiscuity
- pregnancy
- gender identity issues
- suicidal intentions
- self-harm
- physical pain or discomfort
- eating problems
- sleeping problems
- neglect at home
- health issues

Sudden Changes in Behaviour

- more withdrawn, quiet ... even well-behaved
- moodier
- uncharacteristically happy, hyper, giddy
- uncharacteristically down
- more outspoken, hostile
- problems with memory
- changes in general appearance or hygiene

Circumstances

- bereavement (family members, friends, even pets)
- illness (self, family, friends)
- house change
- family disputes
- gangs
- parental separation
- family member leaving home
- poverty

- racial/ethnic/religious issues
- language problems
- break-up of relationship
- involvement in criminality, court appearance
- specific pressures (e.g., examinations)
- failure (e.g., examinations)

Identifying Potential Early School Leavers

The list below is presented as an aid to identifying students who may be at risk of leaving school prematurely. The questions are very frank and open. All items would not necessarily carry the same degree of importance. Neither can we assume that full second-level schooling is necessary or desirable for all students but if students leave early it should not be for any of the following reasons.

School

Does the student dislike the school?
Is the student doing subjects that are need-satisfying?
Are there large variations in test results? This includes profile discrepancies across tests of different variables (e.g., aptitude, achievement) or fluctuations in similar variables across time.
Does the student exhibit any form of learning difficulty (disadvantaged in literacy, numeracy, behind in subjects, hearing or sight problems, inadequate study skills)?
Do many teachers find it hard to like the student?
Is the student often absent?
Does the student present behavioural problems (including withdrawal)?

Personal

Is the student unhappy?

Has the student experienced trauma in recent times? (e.g., bereavement, abuse, parental separation, relationship break-up).
Is the student's cognitive development out of sync with his/her peers? (e.g., ability to plan ahead, take responsibility, locus of control, sensitivity to others)
Does the student lack a goal in life, even a short-term goal?

Relationships

Is there a language, racial, gender or cultural difficulty, including possible prejudice?
Does the student lack friends in his or her class?
Does the student avoid general school activities such as sport, drama, trips?
Are the student's social skills weak? (sociability, assertiveness)
Does the student avoid mixing at break times?

Family

Does the student's family not buy into education (e.g., not showing good involvement with the school, parent-teacher meetings)?
Is the parenting style indulgent, authoritarian or detached?
Is there a history of school-dropout in the family?
Does the student's home neighbourhood have a high incidence of school dropout?
Is the student's family experiencing any form of instability? (poverty, unemployment, bereavement, illness, separation, refugee status, asylum seeking, deportation, prejudice)

Obviously if any of the above characteristics relate to a high probability of school dropout, then countering these will help improve participation in education.

Since dropping out is normally associated with children who are problematic in school, staff do not normally have the interest nor resources to follow up on these cases. However, research into those who have left formal education early could help highlight the deficiencies in our system.

Dystraxia

Schools are much kinder places than they were half a century ago. Allowance is made for the child who has any known disadvantage. Special facilities are provided in class and in examinations for those who are physically impaired, for those whose hearing or eyesight is weak. Those who are identified as slow readers or learners are also given help so that all students can aspire to reach their full potential.

Based on my own experience and observations I believe that there is yet one more group of very seriously disadvantaged students whose problem has not been clearly identified so far and yet what they have may very well be the most serious educational disadvantage of all. This concept is so new that I needed to create a new term for it.

The ability they lack could be called *abstraction* which I choose to define as *the cognitive ability to perceive outside of their present experience*. This lack translates into a form of cognitive blindness or at least short-sightedness, and I have given this condition the name "dystraxia". If a person has not developed this special ability to abstract (and this is through no fault of their own) then there can be very serious consequences at several levels of their life.

Consequences of Dystraxia

SELF: A sense of self relies on being able to reflect on oneself and this in turn requires the person to view themselves from the outside. This is virtually impossible for those who cannot abstract. They will live very much in a continuous present moment; they will be impulsive, even explosive. They will not understand their own emotions very well since that requires some degree of self-awareness that they do not have. Deciding and problem-solving, since these rely on being able to see multiple facets of a situation, will be very difficult for them. They will find it very hard to generalise any learning to other situations.

OTHERS: They will not be able to put themselves in someone else's shoes and so will lack sensitivity to others. Empathy will be very difficult. They will be more likely to be tactless, cruel, to use aggression, to communicate in inappropriate ways. Their relationships will get into constant difficulty. They will not understand rules and regulations nor their fair application. They will often feel "picked on", victimised. They will find it difficult to resolve conflicts. They will find it hard to understand individual differences. They will constantly miss the nuances in adult communications to them.

TIME: A sense of time requires a person to perceive beyond the present moment and so these people will also lack this. They will find it hard and even undesirable to plan.

Tomorrow's homework will not be done because tomorrow does not exist for them. It is not the memory of the past that is flawed but the anticipation of the future. Career planning will not make sense for the same reason.

RESPONSIBILITY: this depends heavily on being able to see one's own behaviour from a broader perspective seeing the longer term consequences of one's actions and taking ownership for them. Without the ability to stand outside of present experience these people will have no sense of a connection between consequences and the behaviour that produced them. They will appear irresponsible, will often do things (e.g., drugs, tattoos, body-piercings, promiscuity, delinquency) with no thought of longer-term consequences. They will not be influenced very much by threats of punishment or jail since the future does not exist for them. They will tend to believe in luck (hence an attraction to gambling), fate, superstitions rather than believe in the value of effort.

In all these areas there is one common factor. People cannot incorporate into their cognition anything that they cannot perceive. They cannot make choices based on what they cannot see in their mind's eye. If we attempt to "correct" such behaviour based on the assumption that they are choosing it with full awareness then our correction is doomed to failure.

Spotting Disadvantages

It is useful for the teacher to know the symptoms and how they point to an underlying disadvantage. Some key aspects of this "mental myopia" are:

- The multiple behavioural and relational problems stem mainly from one deficiency.
- It is not a neurological "defect" or "disorder" but a disadvantage, something they have not developed.
- This developmental inadequacy probably stems from a chaotic childhood.
- It is not a deliberate choice on the part of such children.
- It can be fixed and the sooner the better.
- Punishment or blame will not remedy this.
- We need to recognise, understand and work with it.

General Guidelines

1. Understanding the underlying problem (lack of ability to stand outside immediate experience) will help teachers be more tolerant of such children and that in itself will be an important first step.

2. Visualise this deficiency as a mental muscle that needs to strengthen so that it can reach outside of immediate experience. This will be a slow process beginning with almost immediate experiences and progressing gradually to more distant experiences.

3. Initially in class give these children very short-term projects, something that can be done in a few minutes. Such tasks should be very concrete and with very obvious advantageous outcomes for the student. Draw attention to what is outside of immediate experience. "What are you going to do?" "How will you do it?" "What will this look like when you have finished?" "How did it turn out?" "Did the finished product match what you had in mind at the start?" "How do you feel about how you planned this and carried it out?"

4. It is important that the work is carried out in a caring and collaborative environment. These children need extra doses of good feeling about their expenditure of effort. Working with experience at the outer edge of their mental perceptual range must appear attractive.

5. Generally teachers need to be aware that the ability to stand outside of immediate experience is vital for all students and that the fostering of this ability must permeate our interactions with students. We already do this to a large extent but we must be more aware of the precise ability we are cultivating and how vital it is for overall well-being.

Examples of Specific Exercises

"What if...?" This simple question can encourage young people to look beyond their noses. It can be fun and can help enrich any learning experience and any subject. In Geography, "What if the River Liffey dried up? What would happen around Dublin?" In History, "What if Columbus had never gone to the Americas?" In Science, "What if somebody invented a car that ran on milk?" In Home Economics, "What if the human being had the digestive system of a camel?" In English, "What if the Government banned poetry?" In modern languages, "What if you were only allowed to use 8 verbs, what would they be?" In Art, "What if you were standing at the other side of this still-life arrangement, draw it as it would appear from there (without going there)." In Social Education, "What if people were charged a fee for voting and you could vote as often as you could afford?"

Consequences: Start with any sentence (ideally one relating to the day's lesson material), for example, "I went to Belfast on Saturday morning." The next person must continue "Because of that ..." She might say, "Because of that I missed my extra hours in bed." The next goes on, "Because of that I was not fully awake." "Because of that I got on the bus for Connemara by mistake." And so on. The idea is to develop awareness of consequences. After using some fun situations more serious examples could be used. "The girl started smoking at age thirteen" …. "Because of that …"

Pros and Cons: Take any issue and invite students to make pros and cons lists. For example, a 15 year-old is offered a well-paying part-time job that will require 2 hours work every week-night and 5 on a Saturday. What are the pros and what are the cons of accepting the job? This could be done as a written exercise that encourages every student to think about both sides. It could also become a debate, ideally one where the two teams are asked to switch sides at some point. In an English class students could be asked to make a list of the positive and negative aspects of a literary character, Hamlet for example.

Alternative view-points: Any exercise that encourages the taking of more than one viewpoint should help abstraction grow. Choose a recent football game, for example. How was the final score viewed by each side's supporters? How are you seen by different members of your family? A research study into the ways different newspapers (or political parties) report the same event would be another example.

Thinking challenges: Teasers and puzzles encourage people to think and enjoy thinking. They invite the individual to stretch their minds beyond the obvious:

- What is five fifths of two thirds?
- What can go up a chimney down but cannot come down a chimney up?
- What was the largest island in the world before Australia was discovered by Europeans?
- How many tracks are there on one side of a 12-inch vinyl record? (Answers in the References section at the end of the book.)
- How many different uses can you think of for a brick?
- What song is your favourite as far as the words (lyrics) are concerned? Is it better than any (or all) of the poems in your poetry book? Argue your case.

Summarising: This is a vital skill for studying and yet we sometimes forget to train our students in it. It is a very specific and very useful type of abstraction. A good starting point can be to ask students to identify the most important words (keywords) in a passage. Then encourage them to note how these words might group or link together. Finally show them how to build a structure such as a spider diagram to represent the ideas. A related exercise is to ask them to read a paragraph and then invent a title for it. A similar skill that is equally important is that of over-viewing, creating a quick summary of something before working on the detail.

Giving students real responsibilities.   If the area of control of young people is so safe that they can never make mistakes (and be exposed to the real consequences of those mistakes), they will not be stretching their abstraction muscles very much if at all. An acceptable level of risk is part of any acceptable level of education. A committee that comes together to plan a graduation celebration or to publish a school year-book are good examples of healthy responsibilities.

Conclusion

What is most important in all of this is that teachers, counsellors and parents add a new dimension to their own thought. As well as evaluating school life with regard to relationships, achievement, literacy, numeracy, intelligence, diligence and co-operation it is important for educators to add abstraction. It is not something that will be taught in a lesson or a course but rather through constant exercising of the "abstraction muscle".

Equally important is the need for an improvement in parenting skills so that children will experience less chaos in early life.   These children also need the disadvantage to be recognised as a disadvantage and not as some deliberate defiance of others.

Public Relations and Guidance Counselling

Everyone thinks they know what teachers do during the day though very few outside of education realise just how busy and varied this role is. Even within a school building there are roles which are often totally misunderstood or even unknown. This can be very true about the guidance counsellor.

To the outsider the guidance counsellor's job seems to be quite attractive:

- usually dealing with only one student at a time
- "work" seems to consist in chatting to students
- a flexible time-table mixing group work and individuals
- has out-of-school meetings
- gets away on trips

The reality, of course, is quite different:

- each new student seeking counselling presents the tough challenge of exploring a whole new world. This requires a high level of concentration throughout each counselling session combined with carefully honed sensitivity to the young person's problems
- the "chat" is a highly skilled and responsible interaction that requires a lot of training and experience
- protection of confidentiality adds a stressful dimension, one that needs to operate alongside ethical and legal requirements about reporting and referral
- adjusting to two different relationships to the same students (as a classroom teacher and as a personal counsellor) is difficult especially in more traditional schools
- dealing with a flexible timetable requires a lot of extra work to plan and manage time on an ongoing basis

- out-of-school work means travel, dealing with different groups and leaves less time for work in the school itself
- trips such as visits to further education and training centres requires great organisation and quite a lot of negotiating with staff to release students for the visits
- there are extra out-of-hours meetings and events

A key feature of all support staff work is confidentiality. A guidance counsellor cannot share the stories that are part and parcel of the work. This carries quite a big responsibility and a considerable amount of professional loneliness. Many of the decisions a counsellor needs to take must be made in isolation, at least from staff-room colleagues.

The career aspect of a guidance counsellor's job requires constant updating of information, a massive yearly challenge. Pythagoras' theorem and the Spanish subjunctives do not experience quite the same constant overhaul.

So the job is open to misunderstanding and underestimation. However, the only person who can combat such a deficit is the guidance counsellor him or herself. If we do not supply information to those around us it is only natural that they guess at what we do as best they can. Here are some suggestions about what the guidance counsellor can do.

- At least once a year give a short presentation to staff about the work that is involved.
- Provide an introduction to your work to the parents of new incoming children.
- Ideally have an information brochure that can be given to staff and parents.
- Have a special section of information on the school website.
- Place posters around the school detailing the service that you offer.

- When you organise events such as evening career conferences, tell all staff members about it, put up advance notices about what is taking place.
- After any event, leave evidence such as notices around the school for a few days afterwards.
- Use specially designed appointment slips so that staff get an idea of the numbers of people who visit you.
- Do keep good contact with fellow staff members (e.g., at lunch times) so that you have a chance to inform them and to correct mistaken ideas about your work.
- Be a resource to staff, sharing ideas about dealing with different student behaviours.
- Keep statistical records of the work you do and publish an annual report.

All members of the support team in a school are well-placed to be a major support to school management. We get to know the psycho-social undercurrents of the school environment in a special way. Although there are many aspects of these we cannot divulge to others we can use our experience to help introduce and shape new programmes in the school.

Just as we are careful to spell out the level of confidentiality we offer our students it is equally important to share this information with colleagues. As is the case with ethics in general, it is better to share this type of information before issues arise rather than afterwards. To that end it is a good idea for each support group in a school to have a document about confidentiality and to share and discuss this with colleagues. This will help ease the pressure on individuals when delicate situations come along.

We can also be alert to special pressures that the management team face from time to time and we can place our expertise in counselling at their disposal.

Teachers in general need to invest time in public relations. During the time when teachers are busily involved in their classrooms there are radio programmes out there where teaching is a regular topic of discussion. The comments made often reflect a total lack of familiarity with modern teaching and the modern school. Teachers do not hear the comments and, therefore, cannot give feedback. The result is that both sides continue their way in mutual misunderstanding.

While teachers have unions that can do a lot in the area of public relations, the staff of any one school can do something in their local community. The next chapter includes some ideas for improving relationships with parents. Regarding the community in general a school needs to have regular communications with local media, have open days for the local people, extend open invitations to concerts and other school events. Making school facilities (such as gyms and playing fields) available to local groups helps build good relations.

Parents and Guardians

William Glasser once said that he thought teaching was the hardest job of all. I disagree. I believe that parenting is best placed to claim this title. Similarly I believe that a strong bond between a school and the parents of the students is very important. Parents can benefit from the special experience teachers have of lots of kids and, at the same time, teachers gain from the support of the parents.

It is sometimes said that teachers operate in the place of parents but they cannot do this in isolation from parents. In some way the educational and caring policies of the school need to synchronise with those of the children's own parents or guardians. Similarly, the overall development of our young people needs to take the students themselves into consideration. A team works best when all its members share the same goals and have worked out strategies together.

The challenge of parenting

- Parents and guardians have the enormous responsibility of bringing up children, of catering for their basic physical needs, their development as persons, their general education.
- They do this in the cocoon that is family life. In that sheltered space it is difficult for parents to evaluate the effectiveness of their parenting.
- They have no professional preparation for this almighty task and its daily challenges.
- They have no easy way of knowing if they are being too restrictive or too lenient, too harsh or too relaxed, too possessive or too carefree.
- Neither have they a way of judging the normality or otherwise of their offspring's behaviour.
- They bring up children who are becoming adults in a very different society from that of their own childhood.

- Course and career options today are dramatically different and more numerous than in the past.
- Relationship, sexual and gender issues play a bigger role in teenage society than in the past.
- Television and the Internet open up worlds to the teenager that we were not familiar with as children.
- Young people today have greater opportunities for foreign travel and emigration than did their parents.

If parents cannot cope well with all these areas their offspring will suffer and this will also impact on their school life. The basic cognitive, social and moral development of our students takes place in their homes and those homes need all the support they can get.

I like to remind parents that their teenagers are indeed from another planet. They nod in appreciative agreement. That planet, I go on to explain, has been identified … and they become curious. That planet, I explain, is the earth of the future, a world of new structures, new values, new ways of relating and the teenagers of today are engaged in the first steps of putting that world together.

What parents can do for themselves

- Meet regularly with other parents who have children of the same age and share ideas and problems.
- Organise and attend courses or presentations about parenting.
- Read books about parenting.
- Become familiar with the Internet in general and with social media in particular.
- Consult with the children's teachers who can evaluate a child's behaviour in the light of what is "normal" for that age group.
- Encourage sons and daughters to get experience of other parents, for example, by visiting friends' homes or having them in the family home.

- Be super-protective of the relationship with the teenager keeping it close even if you need to discuss differences.
- Have patience, lots and lots of patience.

What schools can do for parents

- Arrange social events and courses that give parents an opportunity to get to know other parents.
- Organise courses on different aspects of parenting. This is something that parents very much appreciate and is much needed.
- Have special meetings for parents, for example, about new course and examination structures, about further education opportunities, about Internet/phone security.
- Ensure that parents know what is going on at school, its general approach to education.
- Avoid the situation where parents are only invited into the school when there is a problem.
- Have a good parents' association that can give the school support for special events, go on school trips, represent parents' general views to the school.

What parents can do for the school

- Learn about what is happening there.
- Be on friendly terms with staff.
- Provide organisational and catering support for school events.
- Accompany some school trips.

A special family meeting

A special type of meeting with a format we copied from a Mental Health Association template many years ago proved very successful.

Students and their parents are invited to this evening meeting. The students are told that (1) the meeting is aimed at helping their parents understand them better and (2) there will be small group meetings but they will not be in the same groups as their parents.

Volunteers are sought from teaching staff who will act as group facilitators and these are given some basic training in group facilitation.

The evening begins with a registration process at the door. In advance a set of coloured labels are prepared, for example, yellow, red and blue. One third of each colour is marked "M" for mother, another third "F" for father and the final third "T" for teenager.

As family groups arrive, labels are issued in such a way as to ensure that each member of the family will be in a different group and that each group will have a fair mix of mums, dads and teenagers. If possible arrange a gender balance of teenagers in each group.

Initially all are directed to a general assembly area.

At the start time, the event organiser (ideally guidance counsellor or home school coordinator) welcomes everyone, says a few words about the evening's arrangements and then shows a short video. This should be no more than 15 minutes and should portray some typical parent/teenager interaction, e.g., about dress, appearance, study. The more issues it can squeeze into the 15 minutes, the better.

Then all the participants are directed to their small group rooms. For approximately 90 minutes an open discussion is facilitated by the volunteer teacher. The emphasis is on making space for all opinions and for keeping the discussion calm. Because all the participants are from different family groups there can be greater objectivity and respect. All family members soon realise that others have the same or similar problems as themselves.

In the final half hour of the meeting all regroup in the main assembly area and the organiser invites comments on what has been discussed in the small groups.

A meeting such as this can be a remarkably positive experience for all concerned. When the family groups arrive home their can be a lot of further discussion of their quite different group experiences.

A more specialised meeting like the above could be arranged for examination year students. Such a meeting could include a selection of teachers. What tends to happen in examination years is that students are at the mercy of a selection of different agendas. Each teacher focuses on his or her own subject, sometimes issuing disproportionate amounts of homework. Parents want their children to do their fair share of housework and yet this may need some modification in an examination year.

The young people themselves are keen to have leisure time but may need help in striking the right balance. A meeting such as this can help students, parents and teachers work together as a team rather than be operating in different directions.

The Strengths of Guidance Counsellors

Most of this book is geared to the work of the Irish guidance counsellor and, indeed, even a glance at the table of contents will give some idea of the variety of work that is involved in this role. The three main prongs of this work are (1) Personal, (2) Vocational and (3) Academic. In each of these areas the guidance counsellor operates at two levels: (a) guidance to groups or classes and (b) counselling to individuals.

From time to time I hear references to the "European model" of guidance counselling. It is an interesting concept especially since it does not exist. If there is a European model, it is what is actually practised in Europe and not the figment of someone's imagination. Many European countries have no guidance counsellor at all (or "school counselor" as wikipedia [en.wikipedia.org/wiki/school_counselor] would have us believe it should be called though they define the job much as we do). Some countries, such as Finland, have a model very similar to our own.

In the Republic of Ireland we have always been careful to say, "guidance counsellor" and not "school counsellor" or "guidance teacher" since we have always emphasised the combination of a guidance classroom and counsellor office approach, an extremely important dual focus.

Guidance counsellors aim to serve the needs of all students and offer general counselling support to those who require it. Psychotherapy is a more specialised form of counselling and in no way can replace the more generalised work of a guidance counsellor any more than a medical specialist could replace a GP.

I believe that our Irish model of guidance counselling is probably the best in the world. Here is why I believe the guidance counselling role is so valuable and I think guidance counsellors need to become more aware of their strengths and tell more people about them!

THE NORMAL CURVE: We have regular experience of the full range of young people, the full normal curve and not simply the problem cases. Compared to external counsellors we have a better sense of what might not be "normal" when we meet young people. Because our experience straddles both the classroom and the privacy of counselling we are uniquely placed to understand the young population of a school.

ENVIRONMENT: We work with young people in their everyday environment and for a big part of their day. We know how they behave with their peers and teachers, in groups and alone, in work and in play. We learn very early on in our work that most students are very well behaved in a one-to-one situation (as in counselling) but can be quite different in the context of a group.

PRIVATE INFORMATION: The personal details that our young clients share with us give us a very special view of what is happening in the teenage world, a view that may be completely hidden from our teaching colleagues.

ACCESS: We have easy access to peers, teachers, parents of young people, and to sources of extra information about the young people.

LINKAGES: We network regularly with local health services, psychologists, police, primary and other schools, alternative education centres, employment services, youth support services and specialist counselling agencies.

EDUCATION: We are part of young people's educational system with easy access to programmes such as social and health education or the tutorial system where developmental and positive approaches to general personal well-being are possible.

TRAINING: Our training extends beyond basic counselling skills, e.g., psychometrics, career work, academic support, personal well-being.

AVAILABLE: Because of dealing also with career and academic areas young people feel free to visit us without being labelled "problem" cases and without being self-conscious about arranging to see us.

LOCATION: Our office is right there in the school. We are very easily reached without complex bureaucratic hoops or costs.

CONFIDENTIALITY: This is a vital characteristic of our role offering young people adult support in very difficult situations.

CONTINUITY: We do not normally change our positions or roles as often as other professionals and so have continuity of concern and experience. For young people this stability is essential.

REPUTATION: From our general interactions within the school young people can get to know and trust us well before they need us. They can observe how we behave in the classrooms and corridors. They can hear how we talk about important issues before they arrange a private meeting.

EXPERIENCE: Guidance counselling is the oldest organised form of counselling available in Ireland.

CONTRIBUTIONS: We have published books, articles, software, special counselling interventions and other resources.

PROFESSIONAL: Guidance counsellors have professional supervision and regular in-service up-skilling.

ORGANISED: We have a professional organisation complete with its Code of Ethics with an annual conference and general meeting.

Conclusion

At this point the reader is possibly asking why certain topics were not mentioned. Well, there are several reasons. First of all this book did not set out to be a general encyclopaedia of educational matters; secondly, the author could only write about areas he is somewhat familiar with; thirdly, I have dealt with some other topics elsewhere (see References section); and last reason, educational issues go on forever!

A teaching or guidance counselling qualification is only part of a life-long learning process. Continued enthusiasm for such learning is a sure sign of a healthy career choice and hopefully we can always convey that same enthusiasm to those young people who have been placed in our charge.

REFERENCES

Resources listed here refer to ideas or publications mentioned in the book and also include some material of general interest to educators and parents.

Bergman, Jonathan & Aaron Sams.   Flip Your Classroom. ASCD, Virginia. 2012.

Bodrova, Elena & Deborah J. Leong.   Tools of the Mind. Pearson, New Jersey. 2007. (Ideas from Vygotsky.)

Bronson, Po & Ashley Merryman. Nurtureshock. Ebury Press, UK. 2009. (Challenges many ideas we have about bringing up children.)

Bronson, Po. How Not to Talk to Your Kids: The Inverse Power of Praise. www.nymag.com/news/features/27840/index.html

Buck Ph.D. , Nancy S. Why Do Kids Act That Way? Peaceful Parenting, Charlestown.   2009.   (Choice Theory ideas on parenting.)

Clay, Marie M. Becoming Literate: The Construction of Inner Control. Heinemann Education, Portsmouth USA, 1991. (Reading Recovery.)

Clay Marie M. Reading Recovery: A Guidebook for Teachers in Training. Heinemann Education, New Zealand, 1993. (Reading Recovery.)

Clay Marie M. An Observation Survey of Early Literacy Achievement. Heinemann. 2002. (Reading Recovery.)

Crawford, Donna K., Richard J. Bodine & Robert G. Hoglund. The School for Quality Learning. Research Press, Illinois. 1993. (Ideas on Glasser's Quality School approach.)

Dryden, Gordon & Jeannette Vos. The Learning Revolution. The Learning Web, Aukland. 1997. (Challenging ideas on different aspects of education.)

Dweck, Carol S. Mindset: How You Can Fulfil Your Potential. Robinson. 2012. (Important ideas on praise.)

Erwin, Jonathan C. The Classroom of Choice. ASCD, Alexandria. 2004. (Aspects of a Choice Theory approach to education.)

Faber, Adele and Elaine Mazlish. How to Talks so Kids can Learn at Home and School. Piccadilly Press, London. 1995. (An internal control approach to education.)

Faber, Adele and Elaine Mazlish. How to Talk so Teens will Listen & Listen so Teens will Talk. Piccadilly Press, London. 2006. (An internal control approach to parenting.)

Gaffney, Sr. Basil et al. In the Driving Seat. WGII, Dublin. 2006. (A personal well-being guide for students, using Choice Theory.)

Ginnis, Paul. The Teacher's Toolkit. Crown House Publishing, UK. 2002. (Ideas on teaching and classroom management.)

Glasser, William. Choice Theory. Harper Collins Publishers, New York. 1998. (The main text on Choice Theory psychology.)

Glasser, William. Every Student Can Succeed. Black Forest Press, San Diego. 2000. (Aspects of Choice Theory applied to education.)

Glasser, William. The Quality School. Harper Perennial, New York. 1990. (Overview of Glasser's Quality School approach.)

Gordon, Thomas. Teacher Effectiveness Training. Peter H. Wyden, New York. 1974. (Many useful ideas on the teacher-student relationship.)

Greene, Brad. New Paradigms for Creating Quality Schools. New View, Chapel Hill. 1994. (Selection of topics on Glasser's Quality School approach.)

Humphreys, Tony. A Different Kind of Teacher. Tony Humphreys, Cork. 1993. (Psychological aspects of teachers, students and their relationship.)

Kohn, Alfie. Beyond Discipline. Association for Supervision and Curriculum Development, Virginia. 1996. (Challenging traditional discipline approaches.)

Lennon, Brian. Cool Anger Management. Download available from www.wgii.ie (Material for helping young people understand and manage anger.)

Lennon, Brian. Dystraxia. (in preparation)

Lennon, Brian. The Career Handbook. Gill & Macmillan, 1983. (Career text-book for juniors.)

Lennon, Brian. Career & Study Planner. Gill & Macmillan, 1989. (Career text-book for seniors.)

Mooney, Brian (Ed.) Educational Matters Yearbook. Education Matters, Dublin. 2016. (Selection of articles on education.)

Pink, Daniel H. Drive. Canongate, London. 2011. (Focus on the nature of motivation.)

Primason Ph. D., Richard. Choice Parenting. iUniverse, New York. 2004. (A parenting approach based on Choice Theory ideas.)

Roy, Jim. Soul Shapers. Review and Herald Publishing Association, Hagerstown. 2005. (Different aspects of student-centred education.)

Sullo, Bob. The Inspiring Teacher. Funderstanding, New Jersey. 2013.

Vygotsky, Lev S. Mind in Society Cambridge, MA: MIT Press, 1978. (Key text of Vygotsky's ideas.)

Answers to the teasers in the chapter on Dystraxia are: two thirds, an umbrella, Australia and one track.

The Author

Brian Lennon worked as a guidance counsellor in St. Oliver's Community College, Drogheda, Co Louth, Ireland for over twenty-five years. He was also head of the Information Technology department. From 2004 he worked as a psychologist for Co. Louth V.E.C. before retiring in 2009. He is a senior instructor with William Glasser International, the body that represents William Glasser's ideas on Choice Theory psychology, Reality Therapy and Quality Schools.

Born in Co. Down, he was educated in Castlewellan and Belfast before studying in Maynooth, the University of Málaga in Spain, Trinity College Dublin and University College Dublin.

He is a Fellow of the Institute of Guidance Counsellors in Ireland and a Fellow of the William Glasser Institute Ireland. He is also Chairman Emeritus of William Glasser International. He has published two career guidance textbooks, "The Career Handbook" and "Career & Study Planner". In the late nineteen eighties he created and programmed QualifaX, the third-level database of further education courses in Ireland and has programmed a number of other guidance-related utilities.

He has presented and taught in a number of countries including Australia, Canada, Colombia, Croatia, England, France, Ireland, Scotland, Slovenia, Spain and the United States of America.

His interests include sailing, photography and information technology. He is married to Laura and they live in Co. Dublin, Ireland.

Email: dystraxia@gmail.com

Twitter: @dystraxia

Printed in Poland
by Amazon Fulfillment
Poland Sp. z o.o., Wrocław

56846199R00128